In Memory of
My mother
Gladys Bagley

*"The garlic has died
away, but the memory
lives on forever"*

June 6, 1919 – March 25, 1959

Table of Contents

Prologue

It's a beautiful, cool day. After all, it is September, but the sun is shining, no clouds to be seen and a bright future ahead after a lifetime of darkness. After a few bad decisions during my life, I don't have the pleasure of living in a house I can call my own, but this cozy little apartment that I now call home is mine. I love to stand out on the balcony that looks out over the trees, listen to the birds sing and feel the cool breeze brush over my face. The sights and sounds of nature help me forget about my past and reflect on the here and now. The apartment is small with two bedrooms and a bathroom at the end of the hallway. It has a small kitchen but a decent size living space. Perfect for two.

My name is Barbara. I have three children which are all now grown. My oldest two sons, Brad and Allan, have since moved out on their own but I still have my youngest daughter, Angela here with me. When she was born, my husband and I referred to her as our little Angel. Since then, the nickname stuck. Now she's just Angel. She's eighteen years old and had just graduated high school in June. It's 1991. She has a bright future in front of her, if only she can decide the first step to take. She has decided to wait on college till she figures it out. I don't mind if she stays with me a little longer though. Her Dad died many years ago. I never remarried again so without Angel here, I think things would get a bit lonely. Angel in the meantime, is enjoying what life she has left as a teen without any cares before reality catches up to her and she finally figures out what it means to be an adult. Angel is thin which is one of many traits she did not get from me. She has freckles and Auburn hair, which is long, wavy, and always kept in style. She always seems to have a boyfriend and she's a social butterfly, with many friends.

4

The only things she got from me was the freckles and Auburn hair. I however, battled my weight my whole life, and my Auburn hair is tightly curled naturally, preventing me from ever being able to style it.

As I stand out on the balcony, I give away to quiet contemplation. I do some of my best thinking out here. I don't really have any hobbies and as Angel gets older, she spends more and more time away from home. I don't have a lot of friends which I've gotten used to over the years, but I do tend to get bored with only the television to keep me company when Angel is out with her friends. My thoughts have given way to finding a cure for my boredom. I pay my bills from income provided from our lovely government. My late husband spent a long career in the Army before retiring in the early 1970's. When he passed, I was entitled to all his retirement and VA benefits. Even in death, he would take care of me for the rest of my life. But I do tend to get bored at times, so I've been thinking. Maybe I'll get a part time job, just for something to do.

The sliding door opened, and Angel joined me on the balcony. "Hey, what's up Mom?"

"I was thinking about going to the mall. Do you want to go?" I won't tell her my true reason for wanting to go until we get there. Given the life I've led, I always feel that I need approval from those around me when making what I consider to be big decisions. And getting a job to me, is a big decision. Although I have gotten much better at it since becoming a single mom for the third time fourteen years ago. But getting a job is huge for me since it will take me away from home and out there in the community amongst strangers, outside my comfort zone. My boys have been out of the house now for about five years, so it has only been Angel and me. So, her opinion has always meant a lot to me.

"I would love to go!" She said in excitement. Probably because she knows that I will cave and buy her a new outfit while we're there. I had a difficult childhood and so I never want her to want for anything. Of course, I will never let her know that.

We climb into my old Ford which has seen better days and make the 15-minute drive to the Tacoma Mall. We pull into the parking lot and I find a space near the Sears store. I turn to her and say, "I heard that Sears is hiring. I thought maybe I could get a part time job in the stock room or something. After that, we can do a little shopping. What do you think?"

"What made you decide to go to work? We don't need the money, do we?" She asked.

"No. I just get bored sometimes at home while you're out with your friends. This will give me something to do during the day."

We walked together to the human resource office and I got an application, sat down and started filling it out. I saw her just sitting there, patiently waiting and I said, "You know, maybe you should apply too. It would be nice if you had your own spending money and start learning some job skills."

"It would be kind of cool to work at the mall." She stood up to grab an application and we fill them out together. We turned them in to the nice lady behind the desk wearing a blue suit who looks over our applications carefully. She then says, "Would you mind waiting here for just a few moments?" Angel and I just look at each other with curiosity and sit back down. A few minutes later, a tall, distinguished looking man came out of the back office and called Angel to go speak with him. About twenty minutes later, Angel came out excitedly. "He gave me an interview and before I knew it, I was hired! I'll be working in the children's department!" I just smiled at her trying to show that I share in her excitement, thinking, "That figures. The story of my life." Although I was happy for her. I was looking for a boredom cure and all I succeeded in doing is gaining more loneliness while Angel is now working. Maybe I should find a hobby.

"Great! Let's go shopping and get you some new work clothes." I said to her.

After a fun day of shopping and a new wardrobe for Angel, it was time to go home. She has a new job to look forward to and I have a hobby to find.

As we entered the apartment, the phone began to ring. Angel went to her bedroom to try on all her new clothes as I cross the room to answer the phone.

"Hello?" I ask into the receiver.

It was my Dad on the other end. He became a distant father after my mother died and led me down an abusive, horrific path I would much rather forget. We visit him on very rare occasions because I want my children to know their grandpa, but I wouldn't care if I ever see or speak to him again.

"Hi Barbara. I know you didn't expect to hear from me." He said after obvious reluctance to say anything at all.

"What do you want Dad?"

"I have been doing a lot of thinking lately. I'm getting up there in years and it's been getting harder to keep up the house by myself." There was a short pause.

"What are you trying to say?", not sure I want to know the answer.

"Well, I was wanting to ask you how you felt about moving back to the house. You and Angie. You wouldn't have to pay rent, or any other bills and you would really be helping me out." He said followed by silence while I absorb what he's asking of me.

"You know that's a huge request for me. I would have to give it a lot of thought before I can give you an answer. I also need to talk to Angel about this." Maybe my luck will change, and Angel will be against the idea. After all, why would an eighteen-year-old girl with a busy social life and a boyfriend want to live with her mother and grandpa under the same roof? I can't help but wonder if he remembers what he put me through or even believe that any of it was his fault? How can he ask this of me, springing it on us so suddenly?

"I know that we haven't been really close over the years, but I hope you consider my proposal." I can sense a need in is voice to have this request fulfilled but I don't understand his true motivation. I haven't been his favorite person in, well…forever.

"Again, let me talk to Angel. I'll let you know soon." This short conversation had left me exhausted. My mind can't stop racing leaving me feeling light-headed as I gain the courage to talk to Angel about the phone call. I will just pray she will make this easy for me and hate the idea.

I went to Angel's room in the back of the apartment, but she wasn't there. She must have left while I was on the phone. I'll just talk to her when she gets home. I feel a little relieved as this will give me a little more time to think about what I will say.

I've been afraid of my father for so long, but Angel doesn't know anything about that. I've put on a brave, unknowing face at every Thanksgiving and Christmas family get together. Every time we visit him for the sake of

8

my kids, every time he took them on fishing trips, I just smiled, feeling the horrors of my past all over again. In their eyes, he has been nothing but a normal, loving grandfather. But I know better. Is he still trying to break me or is he truly trying to make up for everything he has done?

It's about six in the evening when I hear Angel come through the door. "Angel, can you come into the living room? I have something that I want to talk to you about." She enters the room and sits down on the couch next to me with a worried look on her face.

"Is everything ok Mom?"

"Well, I got a call from your grandpa when we got home. He's worried about living by himself and has asked if we would be willing to move in with him. He pointed out that we wouldn't have any bills to pay so maybe I could save up some money to buy our own house later."

Now why would I say that? It sounds liking I'm arguing why we should do this and not why I think it's a bad idea. I obviously wasn't given enough time to think about what to say. Why did I have to raise a responsible teenager and not one who would predictably come home late while I'm in bed postponing this conversation until tomorrow.

"I told him I'm not making any decisions until I talk to you. What do you think?" Angel doesn't know about my past and how much I despise that house. I'm counting on her teenage tendencies and decide that she doesn't want to give up the social life she has by not only living with her mother, but now her grandfather. I counted on her to say, "I don't really want to." Her response surprises me.

"Well, I like the idea of living in a house with our own front yard. It would also be nice to have more money.

Maybe I can have a dog! I have a car, so I can still go see my friends and my boyfriend anytime I want. I'm leaving the decision up to you, but I would be ok with it whatever you decide." She said.

Wow, not the response I was expecting. I was really hoping she would say no. How can I tell her now, "Never mind, I don't want to live with him?" She would wonder why I even asked. And I risk having to explain to her why I don't want to have anything to do with him. I mean, why would I pass up the chance to live rent free? I just don't think I'm ready for my kids to hear about my past just yet, or ever.

I called Dad back. "Ok, we'll do it, but I have one condition. If I feel that you're treating Angel unfairly or you make her feel unwelcome, we're out of there." I hung up before he could respond. We never have anything to say to each other beyond what needs to be said. Otherwise, it becomes awkward.

My lease just happens to be up at the end of the month. Is it fate that the timing is just so, that I wasn't considered for that job since I will no longer have time for one? Now that I must deal with Dad and take care of his house?

I will go to the apartment manager to give my notice first thing in the morning. Then there will be no turning back. At the end of the month, we'll be homeless if we don't follow through with this. Been there and done that. I would never put Angel through that experience.

****

Within a few short weeks, we were all packed up and ready for our new chapter. There's not a lot of room at the house so most of our furniture had to go in storage. The car is stuffed with only what we need. I'm starting to

10

feel de ja vu as we moved many times when I was a kid with only what will fit in a cupboard in a trailer. I'm hoping that we don't need to be there long. I can feel my nervous heart beating fast, not knowing what to expect. Reluctantly, I start to drive with Angel's packed car following close behind.

We turn onto the gravel road leading to the old house. I feel everything washing over me in slow motion, blood quickly rushing to my head. My painful childhood memories are returning to me. Memories I spent years trying to bury. I pull into the driveway, turn off the car and just sit. The house is just how I remember it. All the times I have brought the kids here to visit, this wasn't home. It was Dad's house. It felt a lot different being here today, ready to move in. But still not ready to call it home. Angel pulls in behind me, gets out and approaches the car. She opens my door, "Is everything ok?"

"Yeah, I just need a moment. Go on in and I'll be along in a few minutes." She turned to go in and announced our arrival to Dad. I stare at the house and I swear I could still see and smell the garlic that long ago bloomed, covering the grounds around the house and my mother holding my hand as we started our new life,

After what seemed like an hour, but only about 5 minutes, I gathered a few things from the car and proceed to go in, meeting Dad at the door. "So, have you figured out the sleeping arrangements?"

The faded green house is small. Three steps into the front door and you're looking at the living space to the left with 2 large picture windows. One window looked onto the front yard and the other into the neighbor's yard. To the right is a corridor to the small kitchen that serves its purpose. Dad had painted all the cupboards and drawers blue and green years ago, but the colors have since faded.

The appliances are the same as they have been for forty years. An old blue a white checkered curtain still hangs over a window that looks out into the driveway under an old carport that hangs out over the kitchen window. A small round table that I remember from many years ago still sits by the front door. Past the kitchen's corridor is the only bathroom in the house with the light switch on the outside which I always thought was an odd place for it. Through the living space is another corridor into another room and yet another one to the right of that room. The two rooms are separated by a partial wall but without any doors. Through the first room is a storage area lined with shelves full of canned food and various other household items. The storage area is the only room in the house with a door other than the bathroom.

Dad said, "I'll convert the back-storage room into my bedroom. You and Angie can do whatever you want to those two areas." Pointing to the two rooms in front of the storage area with the partial wall.

I looked at Angel. "So, which room do you want? No matter what, whoever is in the back room will have to go through the other room to get out. The other option, is we could share the back room for now."

"I guess we could share the room for now. We'll only be in here to sleep." She says. She never ceases to amaze me at how mature she can be at times.

So that's what we did. After a few short days, Dad was in the back room and we were settled. We went outside to the front yard and look at each other. "So now what?" I ask.

She thought about that for a moment and says, "I guess we move on with life. I've got to get ready for work. See you tonight." Then she was gone.

Angel left for work and I now find myself standing in the yard alone, looking at the house. My Dad is sitting in his worn leather recliner in the front room, puffing on his pipe as he has done for years. It's almost as though nothing had happened, but I know better. Memories come flooding back no matter where I look. If Angel wasn't here, I never could have made this step, moving back into a house that I hate so much. A month ago, we were living a happy life with a promising future in an apartment I loved. Now I'm living a nightmare. This could go two ways. Facing my past could help me find closure so I can move on with my life in peace or I can reach the realization that I was never meant to have that peace I've been so desperate to find. The one thing I'm grateful for is that none of my children are aware of the demons in my past and what a horrible man my dad was and maybe still is.

It's ten at night as I climb into bed after an emotional week moving in. I never thought that I would live in this house again. I looked over onto my nightstand and see a picture of Jim, my dear, sweet husband. "How did my life ever come to this? I miss you so much." I then heard Angel come home from work. I pretended to be asleep so that she doesn't see the tears. I close my eyes, eventually drifting off to sleep. My dreams filled my head with a playback of memories. It was as though I was being forced to relive the whole nightmare again in order to make sense of why I had to go through it in the first place. I see myself as a ten-year-old child. We were living the typical life in a military family, moving frequently, whenever and wherever the government told us to. This time, we were told to go to another small town in California called Jolon. I was sad about having to leave my friends and school once again, but we knew that it was part of the military life. We were becoming accustomed to it. It was my Mom, Dad, my sister Jackie and I, but despite yet another move, it was a happier time. We were moving to the last place I would ever find happiness before the real-life nightmares started.

Why do I need or want to tell my story?

Because if it can help just one person along the way, to show any obstacle can be overcome, and to tell anyone who has faced the same kind of torment I have known, "You are not alone." Some say suicide is the easy way out, but I've learned it is not the answer, that any problem can be worked out in time. I am human, complete with flaws, and not the carefree individual everyone assumes I am.

Here's my story as I remember.......

Chapter 1

Jolon, California

1954-1956

I remember Mommy and Daddy. I remember them both as they were, each healthy and vibrant, so much in love with each other and with life itself. I remember myself as a little girl cuddled in my daddy's lap listening to his war stories, waiting for Mom to finish dinner. Listening to her sing in the kitchen as she worked. My sister Jackie doing her homework while she waited for Mom to call us for dinner.

Sometimes I wish for that little girl to return. I miss her innocence and I miss the mom and dad that she once knew. The dad that became so different from the man he was before Mom's death.

I miss California, but I know as much as I want to, I could never return to things as they were. I tried once before to return for a visit to the place where I was the happiest, but everything had changed, as they always do. The friends I remembered had moved on and the buildings were replaced by newer structures. The general store and trailer park had disappeared. I wanted to show my children the places I loved as a child, but everything was gone. Everything but the memories.

We moved to California when I was about ten years old, always traveling from one post to another in our small trailer. Dad would settle us in at a nearby trailer park and we would do our best to make it our home for however long Dad got stationed there.

I never thought I would miss that trailer, but it brought the four of us closer together than I ever thought possible. We lived in close quarters and we had to learn to get along together. The trailer consisted of three small rooms. At the rear was a small bedroom where Mom and Dad slept, with only a curtain to offer their privacy. In the middle was a kitchen with a small refrigerator, butane stove to cook on and a small sink. The front room had a sofa bed, small dining table, and eventually a television. There were four small closets, two on each side of the trailer. We each were issued one closet. Because of the lack of space, we had to keep all our personal belongings in our perspective closets. If it didn't fit, we didn't keep it.

There was no bathroom, so for years we had to use the facilities at the park. There were two shower stalls, two toilets, and a sink. Dad would always try to park near the restrooms so it would be more convenient for us to use. I often wished I could just take a bath in my own home. I hated having to walk the small distance in my robe to the bathroom to take a shower.

I can remember as a small child cuddling into Mom and Dad's bed to go to sleep and being gently carried into the front room later in the evening to sleep on the sofa bed next to my sister.

And I remember Jolon. Not as it was now as I stood beside the sign that said, "Welcome to Jolon", with my children, but the Jolon so many years ago, when I was ten years old.

Jolon, population of about one hundred. Situated on the outskirts of a small army post in California called Fort Hunter Liggett. The town consisted of one general store that included a small restaurant and the trailer park, behind the building. Both of which were owned by one family, whom I didn't know at the time, would become our best friends.

Most of the occupants of the trailer park were soldiers and their families, like us, that were stationed at the post.

At first sight, Mom was horrified because it was isolated among acres of woods with no stores or houses in sight. I was young so the woods excited me. I couldn't wait to settle in and start exploring. It did not dawn on me that there would be no movie theaters, skating rinks, or ice cream parlors, as I was used to in all the other towns where we had lived. I thought about the possibility that there was nothing to do in this small town and I may become easily bored.

We were tired when we arrived in town. I had to use the restroom, so we pulled in front of the store and we all headed inside.

It was a country diner complete with a jukebox that offered mostly country music.

The store's owner, Ramona, came over to introduce herself and take our order. She stood a little over five feet tall, short dusty brown hair, round face, and looked like she weighed close to two hundred pounds.

"Hello, are you new in town or just passing through?".

Dad looked up at her and said, "We actually just moved here today. I want to rent a space for our trailer in the park. I'm stationed at Fort Hunter Liggett."

Anxious to eat I was the first to order, "I'll take a cheeseburger and fries with a soda please." It's been awhile since I had a decent meal and I was starving

Mom, Dad and Jackie ordered lunch as I stared out the window imagining the possibility that this small town held.

"It's my husband Eldon you'll want to talk to about trailer spaces. He'll be here in a moment."

The food tasted delicious, and the service was fast and friendly. The owners made us feel welcome from the first moment we entered. By the time we finished eating, we were more relaxed and excited to begin settling down. After getting acquainted with our new neighbors and landlords, Dad and Eldon left to take the trailer to our spot.

Jackie was as excited to learn Helen, their daughter, was her age. Ramona promised Jackie that Helen could show her where the high school was and help her get acquainted with other teenagers around town.

Then there was Ronnie. I was let down to know they had a son and not another girl my age to play with. Ronnie was also ten. We were at the age when I was happy if boys would keep their distance from me. Ramona called Ronnie out to meet us and I could tell after we were introduced that he'd also rather be anywhere else but here. Little did we know then that we would soon be best friends, inseparable, and I would have my first crush on a boy.

Ronnie was not what you would call handsome, but then at my age all boys looked weird. He had straight brown hair and a round freckled, pimply face. His weight was proportionate to his height.

When we first moved to Jolon, nobody owned a television. Most could not afford such luxuries, so we learned how to keep busy and invent outside activities to do.

Ronnie had lived in Jolon his whole life, so he knew every inch of the woods and was delighted to show me around. Together on our bikes we would pedal for miles, stopping to admire the birds and feed the deer. We would secretly explore the army reservation, knowing we were trespassing. Danger was all around the woods but that only added to the excitement. We would hear the far away guns as the soldiers played their war games, and during deer season the hunters shot at anything that moved. We would discover old hand grenades and leftover bullet shells, deserted in the woods by the soldiers. We would play war games of our own for hours, running from tree to tree as we threw our findings, pretending to blow up the enemy.

Mom started working at the store so Ronnie and I would sneak into the kitchen, grab snacks, help ourselves to the pop and have the time of our lives.

The school we went to was the best school I could ever remember attending. It was a small country school, about twenty miles away. Four grades were in one room and we were all friends. It did not matter who you were, where you came from, or what you looked like. I was not judged for who I was or what I looked like. I was popular and had more friends than I could ever remember having. Even with so many friends, I was still fascinated with Ronnie. He was my idol, the one I dreamed of marrying someday when I grew up. Secretly, I had hoped he felt the same way.

Neither one of our parents ever discussed sex with us. They never worried that we spent too much time together. We were children, and there was nothing to worry about, or so they thought.

I did things at Jolon that I as a mother would punish my kids for, but at the time we saw no wrong. We had hoped are parents would never find out about some of the things we did, but somehow, I believe mom knew and she trusted me.

There was a nearby lake a few miles from the park where the local kids would go to swim. It was a beautiful lake surrounded by trees and rocks. The lake was nicknamed "the GI hole," because it was where many of the soldiers would go to hang out. We just simply referred to it as the swimming hole.

"Hey, do you want to check out the swimming hole? I bet there will be some of the other kids from school there." Ronnie said.

"Sure, let's go."

He led me to the swimming hole where we found a group of kids splashing around in the lake. The lake was not big but it sure was beautiful. I feel a twinge of jealousy seeing all the kids splashing around. It must have been close to one hundred degrees and that water looked so refreshing. That's when I noticed that their clothes were spread around the edge of the water.

I looked at Ronnie, "Why are they all naked?"

"None of the kids around here care what each other looks like. It's just easier to throw your clothes off and jump in when you want to go for a swim instead of changing into a suit. We're all friends here." He explained.

This concept was new to me. I never imagined undressing in front of other people at any of the other places I have lived. Especially in front of other boys. I've had a weight problem all my life. I didn't even want to see myself naked. After some persuading, I soon joined in. It looked like fun and I was hot. I didn't want to be left out

After I was first introduced to the lake, we would ride our bikes there on hot days. We never took our swimming suits with us because we swam in the nude. Sometimes it was just Ronnie and me and on occasion, other kids from school would join us. We never thought about being naked, swimming for hours and swinging from tree branches into the water like Tarzan.

One game Ronnie and I played often was spin the bottle. There was an abandoned trailer in the park where we would go for our game. I liked that game the best because it would be just the two of us. We would take turns spinning the bottle, shedding a piece of clothing each time one of us lost until we were both naked. It was different when we were in the trailer than at the lake. We were silent as we stared at each other's bodies, sometimes touching, but never anything more. We were finally learning what our parents never explained to us before. The difference between boys and girls.

I remember when the first television entered the park, and it was in our trailer. Dad decided to surprise us. Even though we could only get one station, it was the talk of the park. Everyone wanted to see our television. The trailer was too small to have company inside, so we created our own "drive-in theater". We would open our front room curtain and window and put chairs outside in front of it. Anyone who wanted to see our television could sit out there and stare through the open window. Popcorn would be served to everyone. All my friends would suddenly be at my place and before long, parents in the park had to listen to their kids complain about why they couldn't have a television too. After the newness wore off and the lack of television shows became boring, we found we preferred going to the lake.

Jackie met a boy from school and fell madly in love. We hardly ever saw her. His family had a farm a few miles away and Jackie stayed there most of her free time. During her courtship I made her life miserable, as most younger sisters do.

I read her diary and snuck around to spy on her dates. I used to keep track of the times they kissed and report back to Mom. She would gently lecture me about tattling and tell me to leave Jackie alone, but it was one game Ronnie and I both enjoyed; spying on our sisters. Jackie would always get even as most sisters do. One day she was target shooting with a BB gun and "accidently" hit me with a pellet after I teased her about her boyfriend. I was not seriously hurt but to this day, it remains in my shoulder as a reminder. I never let her forget that day. We both laugh about it now, but it wasn't funny at the time.

When I was almost twelve Ronnie and I became steadies, but each had a different version of how that happened. I remember Ronnie asked me if I wanted to wear his ring as a reminder that someday we would be together forever. Ronnie said I tricked him, taking his ring without his knowledge and started wearing it. But no matter what, I had the ring and Ronnie was too polite to ask for it back. I was the envy of all the girls at school.

I hoped with all my heart that Dad wouldn't get stationed anywhere else. I didn't want to move ever again. I was happy and had lots of friends. I could see that Mom was happier at Jolon than any other place we've been as well, but it had already been two years. Longer than any other assignment Dad has had before, so we knew it was only a matter of time. July 1956 Dad received his orders. We were headed to Fort Lewis, Washington.

Jackie was eighteen by then and engaged to be married so she chose to stay behind. The three of us packed our belongings. It was time to leave once again. Saying goodbye to Ronnie was the hardest thing I ever had to do. I cried and we hugged as friends, both of us knowing we would probably never see each other again. I reached around my neck, removed Ronnie's ring from the chain I wore it on and put it in his hand.

"You were right, Ronnie, I did take your ring. This belongs to you; I'll never forget the time we had together."

I looked back in the rear window of the car as we drove away. I saw Ronnie wipe a tear away as he waved goodbye. We were leaving the home we had known for two years and the future of uncertainty, not knowing then that none of us would ever be the same again. Not realizing that I had begun my journey onto a long and winding road into a future of darkness

Chapter 2

Our New Home - Parkland, Washington

1956

The trip from California to Washington seemed to fly by. Dad drove straight through Oregon and into Washington. It felt strange to be in the back seat alone without Jackie next to me. I slept most of the way and before I knew it, we were there. Despite what I heard about the constant Washington rain, the sun was shining, welcoming us to our new home.

We found a trailer park that rented by the day and pulled into a spot near the bathroom as always. It was a small park situated just outside of Tacoma.

Dad had thirty days before he had to report to work. He had always promised Mom he would get her out of the trailer and buy her the house she had always wanted. He was nearing the end of his Army career and decided Washington is where he wanted to settle down. Therefore, while Mom once again set up our things, Dad went out to find us a house. A place we could finally call home.

I was almost as excited as Mom. I would miss the trailer but at last we would have a bathroom and I would have a bedroom of my very own.

Money was tight so we couldn't afford much. Imagine our surprise when Dad came home and said, "I found a great deal on a house. I can't wait for you to see it!"

Nervous about what kind of great bargain he found, we were off to see our new home.

24

We got into the car and headed for the treasure Dad had unearthed. The house that we would now call our home for the next several years. I couldn't believe that Dad went ahead and bought a house without letting Mom go along much less letting her have a say in such a big decision.

Though she didn't say anything, I could see the disappointment in her eyes. She was looking forward to picking out her new home.

"There it is!" he exclaimed.

We saw it, but we didn't believe it. Was this a joke? What was Dad thinking, had he lost his mind?

It was on a dead-end road shared by only one other house. The road was gravel with a creek on the right side surrounded by blackberry bushes. On the left was our house! Mom's eyes teared up as soon as Dad pointed it out, but he didn't even notice as he looked very pleased with himself.

Mom didn't want him to know that she hated it. We didn't even have to look at the inside. What we saw on the outside was enough. The house was barely visible from the road because the front yard was overgrown, not with weeds as one would expect, but with garlic! Bush after bush of garlic. Some were up to my waist. The garlic was ripened so while other yards smelled of roses, our yard smelled of garlic! And to this day, whenever I see garlic, I see our house as it was on that day. It was a one-story shack with no foundation which caused it to lean. We walked around to the back in order to delay seeing what lies inside waiting for us. The back yard was quite big, surrounded by blackberry bushes to let us know where our property ended. And more garlic was growing in the back yard! Where there wasn't garlic there was pieces of rotted lumber, old toilets, a bathtub, and car parts strewn about. It reminded me of the city dump!

At last the front door was unlocked to disclose the front room. There were two picture windows with most of the glass broken. It was small and looked like we could barely fit a couch in it. To the right was a kitchen that only one person could fit into comfortably. Off from the front room, next door to the kitchen, was the bathroom. The toilet was the kind you flushed by pulling a chain attached to the ceiling. The bathtub was on four legs and rusted in spots, looking like it was ready to fall through the floor. As we walked through the front room, I noticed peeling, faded wallpaper on every wall.

We entered the master bedroom which you could see from the front room because there were no doors to offer privacy. As a matter of fact, there wasn't one inside the whole house except for the bathroom. The bedroom didn't have a closet. No carpet, only bare wood on the floors and cracked windows. Just one wide open space. Was there only one bedroom? Did Dad forget about me? Where was I going to sleep? These questions were answered before I could put them into words. Dad pointed to the right to a cubby hole not much bigger than a closet. I wondered if I could even fit a small bed in there. It looked like there would be no privacy because, again, there were no doors.

"First thing I'll do is put up a wall to separate your room from ours, Barbara," Dad informed me. Fine ---- but that still meant I would have to go through their room to get to my "bedroom"!

I was already longing for our trailer back, and wishing we were back in Jolon away from this strange town and horrible house! I could tell by Mom's expression that she was wishing for the same thing. We both thought Dad had lost his mind!

The house next door was a single-story rambler, older but nice. A beautiful porch swing was in the yard and a rather large garden in back. A very well-kept house. I wondered just who lived there. And I secretly wished that was our house instead of this dump!

As I stood in the yard recalling that first day, I could almost feel Mom beside me, shaking her head at Dad. As I looked at the house, I thought I smelled the garlic blooming, though that was long gone and replaced by grass. Nothing else changed much. Dad was always talking about the changes he was going to make, but I could not tell much difference. The house still leaned, and the shingles were still hanging. The door he promised me in my bedroom, a curtain hung instead.

I looked at the large maple tree in the front yard, waving ever so slightly in the breeze, hovering over the house, shadowing it from the sun. I recalled the day Mom planted that tree. It was the day we moved into the house and it was the only thing left of her. Everything else that she had planted was removed. The tree remained, full of life, and I had the feeling that if the tree continued to grow and live, Mom would be with me. The tree was a symbol of the faith, hopes and dreams Mom had that somehow would carry me through.

Chapter 3

Franklin Pierce, High School

1957-1962

It had been over thirty years since we lost Mom but to me it was only yesterday.

Mom was not a pretty woman, just average, but she was a beautiful person. Finding good in everyone came easy to her. Most say I look like Mom. Auburn hair, freckles, round face, tipping the scale at two hundred pounds. She had straight, thin hair, unlike the thick, natural curly hair that I inherited from Dad.

Mom grew up in South Dakota, with four sisters and four brothers. As was told to me, two of her sisters, Mae and Stella, decided to head west after graduation. So, without any definite plans, they hitch-hiked cross country to Portland, Oregon. Mom promised she would join them when she finished school. She saw no future in South Dakota so in keeping with her promise, Mom moved to Portland, Oregon in 1940.

Mom found work as a cocktail waitress in a lounge. That's where she met Dad. He stopped in for a drink with some army buddies. From the moment they met, they knew they were meant to be together and were married two weeks later.

I remember Dad in his Army uniform, always standing at attention, with a pipe in hand and black curly hair, standing at about five feet 8 inches tall and 150 pounds.

Mom was the center of my life. She was not just my mother but also my best friend. We became even

28

closer after leaving Jackie behind in California. Mom doted on her two girls, so when she had to leave my sister behind, it tore her apart. The love she had divided between us suddenly was lavished upon me.

To say that Mom was a generous person is an understatement. Mom loved to bake but she seemed to forget there was just the three of us at home. She baked enough to share with the neighbors for years and she did. The aroma of pies and cookies filled the house, and during blackberry season she'd be at the creek picking enough berries for cobblers, pies and lots of canned jelly. From the time I could remember, I was helping Mom in the kitchen, sometimes getting in her way, but she never chased me out. When Mom wasn't in the kitchen you might find her at her sewing machine making me a new dress, using the last of her materials on me while she did without. Not to mention any strays that always seemed to find our house. They knew they could get a handout. Whether it be a dog, cat or a hungry child, Mom was there to feed and nurture them.

I could always count on Mom to volunteer as a helper at school, being active in PTA and going to all my school activities, including helping on many field trips. There were many times when Mom was sick and should have been in bed, but she never let me down, forcing herself to go, always with a smile.

School was so different in Washington than the small country school I last attended in Jolon. Before we moved, I was one of the popular kids in school. Everyone seemed to get along great regardless of the way they looked or the style of clothes they wore, but after the move, things suddenly became different.

While Mom was with me, she made it bearable to deal with the daily problems of life at Franklin Pierce. I had someone to confide in when things went wrong, someone who understood the frustrations I was going through at starting a new school.

It was a large school comprised of both Junior High and High School students; a section of the school having been set aside for the youngest grades. It was fall of 1957, I was twelve years old and I was just starting the seventh grade.

There I was, starting a new school without a single friend, striving to be noticed. I felt like an outsider looking into a world I yearned for. I wanted friends and the popularity that others found so easy to obtain. The tension I felt the first day of school, with Mom by my side, heading for the office to register. Eyes were staring at me as we passed. The comments I overheard gave me an uneasy feeling, "look at the new kid." Whether Mom heard them or not, she didn't let on. I knew that attending this huge school was going to be HELL! I wanted to run the other way, but we kept walking to the office and before I knew it, I was officially enrolled. My life was about to change forever.

I was born back when parents would often say, "Remember there are starving kids around the world." As if they all got together to find ways for us to finish our plates. When it was common to see overweight mothers enforce the same punishment on their children. Where familiar smells of home baked goodies filled the kitchen in every home in America. Where the word diet was unthinkable. Where a starving child was an unhealthy child.

I was overweight most of my life. Big boned Mom called it. I didn't think my weight was a problem until I hit those terrible teens. Where girls noticed boys and yearned to be noticed back. Where proms were only for those with dates. Where you dared to not go solo to dances. Where only the pretty and thin were chosen. Where I closed myself in my room and cried because I was one of the un- chosen few.

Mom was always fighting my battles for me. It seemed as if something occurred each week that sent her rushing to the principal's office. Kids teased me about my weight and homework was missed because someone would tear it up or destroy my books.

Many times, she would march into the principal's office to complain.

"I'll look into it" was his reply. But he never did. Or at least it didn't appear so as nothing ever changed.

"Stick and stones will break my bones, but names will never hurt me." Whoever made up that saying must not have been picked on. Names do hurt and last a lifetime. Bones will eventually heal.

One incident I remember as if it were yesterday. It was the last day I ever rode the yellow bus home from school nearing the end of eighth grade and the last year Mom was with me. There were no seats available that day, so I had to stand in the aisle for the short ride home. Kids were seated on all sides of me. The kids who I had most of the problems with.

"Hey fatso!" or "Dummy failed her test today". It went on and on.

I didn't respond, pretending that they were speaking about someone else as I fought back the tears. I would not give them the satisfaction of seeing me cry.

"Hey, I'm talking to you" Nancy said.

Nancy! The leader of the pack. For years my tormentor. I never could figure out what Nancy had that made people listen and do as she commanded. She was not a pretty girl. She had short straight black hair and was one of the smallest girls in school. Nancy never seemed happy, except when she was picking on me. I never remembered a time when she ever smiled. Her grades were average, and she was in many of the school clubs. For some reason, as tiny as she was, the others seemed afraid of her. Afraid to stick up to her. Even the boys followed her around like sick puppies, always trying to please her, even if it meant tormenting me.

On this particular day, Nancy decided to try a new tactic. She grabbed my books and started tossing them to the other kids. Back and forth, papers flew everywhere. Pages ripped from the books. Books that would probably have to be replaced by my parents. I made an effort to try and grab my books, but it was fruitless. The bus driver continued driving, not attempting to help me. Even he seemed to stay out of Nancy's way.

At last we were at my stop and I was one step closer to getting home. The door opened and I stumbled out. The fun was over for the kids, so they tossed my damaged books out after me. I was crying when I entered the house and told Mom what happened. Back into the car we went. Mom was going to have it out with the principal!

She ranted and raved. I can't remember ever hearing Mom raise her voice like that before. She told him he wasn't doing his job if the kids behaved like they did. What happened after that astounded me. You would think that as a principal he would have talked to all the kids involved. Wrong! He implied that maybe, just maybe, I did something to cause it. And maybe I should consider not taking the bus anymore! Well, one thing he said that we listened to… I no longer rode the bus! I lived four miles from school, but I walked it every day from that day on!

There was a handful of kids who were cast aside. They were the "Nothings". Both ignored by the teachers and kids alike. They were the ones with grades just above passing. Most had weight problems or hand-me-down (not hip) clothes.

Since the first day of school I was classified with the group of "Nothings"

We didn't have the money to buy nice clothes. If Mom didn't make what I wore, then it came from thrift stores. My weight problem didn't help matters either. No matter how hard I studied, I was lucky to get a passing grade.

The kids were cruel beyond reason. Not a day went by that we didn't suffer the humiliation of being tormented by the "in" crowd. Name calling and practical jokes became everyday occurrences for the "nothings." It was inevitable that we would seek out each other for friendship.

Rose was one of us, one of the nothings of the school. Being alike in many ways, we became instant friends. Her parents were divorced, and she lived with an abusive father, never having known her mother. Like me, she couldn't afford nice clothes and she, too, had a weight problem.

Rose, standing just over 5 feet tall, long straight dirty blond hair, she weighed close to one hundred and fifty pounds

Sometimes I was thankful for my life and to not have hers. Rose had another sister and a brother, but she was the oldest. Several times, they were removed from their home and place into foster care. That was when their father was drinking too much or sexually abusing his daughters. Rose's younger sister was sexually assaulted by him many times but was afraid to speak up. Many times, their dad tried things on Rose, but she'd always back away and turn him in, knowing she'd have to leave until he got help. They were always placed back into the home.

On one occasion, Rose's dad even offered me some money if I would sleep with him! I was shocked and told Rose. She snickered and replied, "Think nothing of it. That's just his way. If he gets what he wants from his daughters, he'll leave you alone."

I was shocked by her statement. From then on, I made sure I was never alone with her father.

We had each other to confide in and cry with. To dream of the day when we would be grown up and on our own.

From the first day we met, Rose was at my house more than hers. To Mom, Rose was another stray who needed love and became the mother she never knew. When things became unbearable at school, Mom was there to comfort us both.

Chapter 4

Good-bye Mom

1959

Mom only lived in her house for two years. The doctors told us that her kidneys were failing and that it was only a matter of time. There was nothing they could do.

Knowing the end was almost here, tears streamed down my cheeks. The only person who ever cared about me was being taken away. Mom was always there to protect me, but I knew that soon I would have to do it alone. Life wasn't going to be the same without her.

I hated seeing Mom in pain. She looked so fragile lying there and I was feeling a little guilty. I couldn't help but think of myself, forgetting about the pain that Mom was going through. Soon it would be just Dad and me and that thought scared me. I didn't know if I could handle living alone with him.

As if Mom could see in the future, her last words to Dad will be forever imprinted on my mind.

"Please take good care of Barbara. She has always been afraid of you and you will need to see through her fears and help her go on without me. I love you both, but we will be together again, until then please be happy."

I never told mom about the fears I had about Dad. I tried to hide my thoughts from her, so how did she know?

As Mom's life came to an end, I knew things were going to be different. Changes were going to be made that would affect the rest of my life.

It was spring of my fourteenth year. Through the window of the hospital room, I noticed the flowers were starting to bloom. The trees displayed several shades of green, proudly swaying in the wind. I was watching two robins singing their songs and hopping from limb to limb, free, without a care in the world. As my mother lay behind me fighting for her life, I found my thoughts straying to better times.

Times filled with happiness, before Mom's illness. A time before we moved to Tacoma, when my sister was home and I was a little girl heading off to kindergarten, decked out in my beautiful dress that mom had made just for me.

If I could only turn the clock back to that time which had passed and start all over. A time when Mom was healthy, and we could once again be a whole family.

As the memories of the past swept over me, the present came rushing back. There I was, next to Dad, sitting next to Mom's hospital bed as she drew her last breath. The tears flowing like never before. Reality hit me like a freight train. Mom was gone. My protector, my confidant, my best friend, a woman so full of life, laid there lifeless.

****

Rose cried with me through Mom's illness and death. She felt as if she lost her own mother. Without Rose there to talk to, I don't know what I would have done.

Thinking back, I couldn't recall a time when Dad ever had a kind word for me. Sometimes I wondered if he was capable of loving anyone but Mom. He always managed to pick out all my faults and keep after me for those, instead of praising me for my good qualities. He was constantly telling me how dumb I was and that I wouldn't amount to much, reminding me every day that I was fat and ugly. That no man would ever want me. Eventually I started believing it.

The night Mom died will always be with me. I know Dad truly loved Mom, and I realize that everyone deals with grief differently, but the way Dad handled it was beyond reason.

Suddenly in his eyes, I was a replacement for Mom, both mentally and physically, starting with the eve of her death. I was in bed, but not asleep. Mom was gone, and I found myself in bed thinking of her. The lights were out, and it was quiet. I heard my bedroom door open and Dad entered the room whispering my name. I did not want to talk to him, so I pretended to be sleeping. Soon I felt him climbing into my bed. I could feel his bare skin next to mine. Though I couldn't see him I could tell that all he was wearing was his underwear. I felt the hardness of him poking at me, all I wanted was for him to leave. He whispered my name a few more times. I was too scared to answer, nor did I want to. I slowly felt his hand pushing up my nightgown, caressing my buttocks and my breast. His penis was hard and pushing out of his shorts. He was rubbing it against my skin.

I was afraid to move or scream. Who would hear me? So, I lay there still pretending to sleep, hoping he would get up and leave. Finally, what seemed like hours, but only minutes, he got up and walked out of my room.

I tossed and turned all night, dreading having to face him the next day. When I climbed out of bed in the morning, he was gone. A note I found on the refrigerator door said that he was out planning Mom's funeral. He wanted me to straighten the house because out of town company was expected.

"Did I imagine the night before?" I thought. Was Dad in my room, or was I dreaming? It seemed so real.

The next week was so hectic that I didn't have time to think about it. I pushed it into the back of my mind, hoping it was, after all, a dream.

Why Dad insisted on Mom being buried near her sister, Stella, and not close to us I never understood. I was too young to voice my opinion, so we drove two hours to Longview, Washington for the funeral. It would be too far away for me to visit Mom, or to bring her the flowers she dearly loved. I wanted Mom close to me, but in my heart, I knew she was with me no matter where her body lay. The service was beautiful. My grandma flew in from South Dakota to see one of her children buried. As I hugged Grandma, I thought I felt Mom's arms around both of us, telling us that everything would be okay. The church was filled with family and friends, who came to say their final good-byes. Mom was so beautiful lying there in the casket. She looked like she was just sleeping. Her hair was done in a style I had never seen her wear before, and she wore a new dress. I wondered about the dress. I had never seen it before and was curious as to where it came from. I can't remember Mom ever having a new dress before, I felt a little bitter now, someone did something for her in death that they would not do for her while she was alive.

After the funeral and the house was once again empty, the dream suddenly pushed forward. I looked at Dad in a new light and I couldn't get rid of the thought that he really did come into my room that night. I was on edge most of the time and couldn't stand being alone with him. Several times dad would "accidently" walk into my room or the bathroom without knocking. He would catch me half-dressed and I could see the look in his eyes before he would apologize and leave.

He would brush up against me while I was in the kitchen or watching television. If I was sitting on the couch, I'd feel his hand reaching for me and I would jump up and leave the room.

Then there was the day I knew Dad wanted me to take Mom's place. I was sitting on my bed listening to the radio when he entered.

"I want to talk to you Barbara"

The tone in his voice told me that it was more than talk he wanted. "or was I jumping to conclusions?" I thought to myself.

"It's been a while since your mom has been gone and I'm awfully lonely. A man needs a woman. I loved your mom, but I can't be alone."

I just stared at him, not knowing what to say. What did he mean it's been a long time since Mom has been gone? It had only been two months!

"You're the lady of the house now and I need you to do the things that your mom once did." Dad reached for me, but I jumped off the bed.

"I have to go Dad. Rose is expecting me at her place." I had to get out of there!

"That will keep. I need to talk to you now!" I could tell by the tone of his voice that he meant for me to stay. "I never ask you for much, but this is important to me." What could I say? He was not the man I knew all my life as Dad. If ever I needed Mom more, it was now.

"You are fourteen and it's time you learned about sex. I'd rather be your teacher, then have you learn it from some boy at school and end up pregnant."

He grabbed for me. I shivered and backed up against the wall. I had no place to go. I could scream, but who would hear me? And if I didn't do as he asked, what would happen to me. Where would I go?

"Your mother was sick a long time. I have been without a woman for months."

"Dad please let me go. We can forget this ever happened!"

He reached one hand out and I felt him touch my breast. I was wearing shorts, making it easy for the other hand to grab my bare leg. I was trapped, and there was no reasoning with him. He grabbed my hand forcing it between his legs. "Doesn't that feel good? That is how a man should feel when he is getting the love he needs."

He was wearing tight fitting shorts and I could see his manliness bulging out. Though I tried to hold it back, I started to cry. "Dad, please don't!"

"Quit crying like a baby!" he yelled, "I am here to teach you to be a woman."

He pushed me to the bed panting heavily and started to pull my blouse off. By then I started fighting back. I didn't care what he did to me, but I was determined to get away. I'd rather him kill me than do what he is planning at that moment. Suddenly he stopped. Stopped as suddenly as he started. He stared down at me, half dressed, and muttered. "Oh God, what am I doing?"

He got up and rushed out of the room and into the bathroom. I heard sobbing on the other side of the wall. My dad was crying! I can't explain why he suddenly came to his senses, but I was grateful he did. I can't begin to think what would have happened had he not stopped.

That night was not mentioned again. Dad was away from home most of the time as if he was trying to avoid me. When he was home, I would go to Rose's house. Anything was better than being alone with Dad. I was afraid he might lose control again. "What if he didn't stop next time?" I wondered.

Luckily there was not another time. Partly because we did not see each other much, but mostly because Dad found a new hobby. Writing letters to women who advertised for men in a singles magazine. Soon our mailbox was flooded with letters from lonely widows. Dad was determined not to be alone and for me to have "proper" supervision while he was at work. He spent hours writing letters, not to mention the long-distance phone calls.

Finally, Dad narrowed it down to one person. A woman from California who was a live-in housekeeper and nurse. Gail! A name I grew to despise. They talked of marriage, perhaps the next year. I couldn't believe Dad would marry someone he only met in letters and knew absolutely nothing about!

Mom was only gone a few months when Rose told me that she had to leave school. Another person in my life was being taken away from me. We were just finishing our eighth year of school and was looking forward to being in high school together. Her dad's abuse was getting out of control and the state was taking her away to a foster home for no telling how long. She promised she would be back some day.

Summer was three months away. I didn't know which was worse. Being in school alone or facing the summer all day at home with Dad.

Gym was the hardest to get through. I hated taking showers with the other girls. As soon as I undressed the snickers would begin. I started making excuses for not showering.

One day as I sat alone on the bleachers, trying to summon the courage to go home, I heard a friendly voice. "Is something wrong?" Startled, I turned to see who was speaking. I didn't know anyone was there. This was the first person to speak to me since Rose left. Realizing I was crying, I quickly wiped my eyes as I looked at the face behind the voice.

"Dear can I help you? You seemed troubled about something"

I recognized the girl. We had talked a few times. I knew her name, but I did not know much about her. Bernice remains my very best friend to this day. I never understood why she wasn't with the popular groups. Bernice was pretty. She had a beautiful singing voice. She had performed several solos in choir and had sung in a few assemblies at school. She was shy and her grades were below average. That alone could cast you aside from your fellow classmates.

Bernice saw that I was troubled that day and she reached out her hand in comfort. But she didn't have to say anything. I felt better just knowing she cared.

Chapter 5

Stranger on the phone

Summer 1959

It was June in my fourteenth year. Mom had been gone for three months at the time, and I still missed her terribly. There was no one to talk to or anyplace to go. I tried keeping busy and out of Dad's way as much as possible. I was unable to forget his past actions and the tension was strong between us.

School was out and the days grew warmer. I just knew that this summer was going to be a long, lonely one. For the first time I would not be spending it with Mom.

I remembered summers past, when I would spend the days with her, baking, sewing and watching our favorite shows on television. She was gone now and there was nothing to occupy my time.

Dad went to work every day, leaving me to the housework. I was young and I should have been enjoying summer. I had very few friends and nowhere to go. I didn't mind tending house. It made me feel grown up and I felt closer to Mom, going through her cupboards and reading her cookbooks.

Bernice would call me every day and we would talk for hours. We seldom could get away from home so our only contact with the outside world was through the telephone line. I really looked forward to our chats. Even though Bernice was a new friend we quickly became confidants. I felt there wasn't anything I couldn't tell her.

Monday, June twentieth started out like any other day. I rushed through the housework and at noon turned on the television while eating lunch. At twelve-thirty the telephone rang. Bernice usually called me at this time, so I picked up the phone and playfully said, "About time you called."

I waited but all I heard was heavy breathing. After a few seconds I slammed the phone down.

"It had to be a wrong number." I said to myself. Thinking nothing of it I finished my lunch.

One hour later the phone rang again. Forgetting about the previous call I picked up the receiver.

"Who is this? Hello?" I was getting frightened now.

One time could have been an accident, but not twice. Whoever was calling wanted to scare me and he was doing a good job. Again, I slammed the receiver down. Twice more the telephone rang, one hour apart. I was tempted not to answer it, but I was afraid Dad would call. Each time the phone rang, all I could hear was breathing sounds.

That evening I was distant, my mind wondering to the phone calls of that day. I couldn't tell Dad. Since Mom's been gone, he had been in his own little world. I should have told him about the calls, but something held me back. The next few days the calls continued. Always when Dad was at work and I was alone, as if whoever was calling could see me through the window and knew what I was doing. After several repeated calls, a man's voice finally broke the steady sounds of heavy breathing.

At first, he just said a couple words. His voice was deep sounding. I hung up right away.

He called back. "What are you doing today babe?" or "Oh, you turn me on." By this time, I was really frightened.

"What if he knows where I live?" I thought to myself. I was really scared and knew it was time to tell someone.

I waited for Dad to come home from work. I knew I had to tell him. The phone rang a few times, but I ignored the steady ringing. I tried to keep busy so that the time would pass.

I wanted to tell dad, but hesitated. "Was I making too much out of those phone calls? Would Dad believe me?" What could he do, short of changing the phone number?

Dad listened, and I could tell he thought I was making more out of it than there really was. I finally convinced him to call the police. I really didn't think that would do any good, but any help would be better than another day of hearing that man's voice! I was upset because Dad acted like this was a way for me to get his attention! I really thought by telling the police it would be over, but it was just the beginning ......

The police wanted me to go along with the caller, to answer the phone and pretend to like his suggestive remarks. The idea was for me to arrange a meeting with him. To bring him out in the open to be caught. I was fourteen! And they wanted me to listen to that filth! The thought of having to do it, but the calls had to stop! It was hard to believe the police would ask for me to go along with this plan, but even harder to believe that Dad would agree to it as well.

A second phone line was installed that was directly connected to the station, so the calls could be monitored. It was bad enough that I had to go along with these calls, but the idea of someone listening in was even more frightening.

By the next day the line was in place and the waiting game began. Twelve o'clock came and the phone rang. He never failed to begin his torment at the stroke of noon. Today was no exception.

Officer Corelli was there by my side and instructed me to pick up the phone.

"Hello" ….

"Why haven't you been answering my calls, Bitch! I know you were home. I don't like being put off!"

"I'm sorry. I didn't know it was you." His breathing was heavy, and the tone of his voice told me he was upset.

"That's ok this time, but don't you ignore my calls again!" He hesitated a moment. I glanced at the officer on the other line. With his nod of approval, I continued.

"Why would I do that? I enjoy your calls, in fact …."

"Shut up!" He interrupted impatiently. "I didn't call you to pass the time of day! Do as I say. Remember, I know where you live. I can tell if you're not following my instructions!"

"I got to go but you better answer on the first ring next time." He immediately hung up the phone as if someone had interrupted the call, and he had to make his escape. Did he suspect that the line was being monitored?

I was shaking by the time I hung up hoping it would be over today. It looked like it would be drawn out to a final climax of the callers choosing. It was hard on me to listen to such filth. Also, I couldn't understand why any parent would allow his child to go along with such a scheme.

"Hello Babe!" The familiar voice rang out the next day. I was beginning to hear those words in my sleep now.

46

I was determined for this to end. "That's better. I like my gals to obey. You are my gal, aren't you?"

"Of course, I am."

He interrupted me sharply. "It's time to get down to business! We have been pussy footing around for a week now getting to know each other. From now on …. listen and do everything I ask of you. Step by step!"

My heart stopped. I wanted to run. I wanted by mom!

"Do you have a telephone in the bedroom?" Glancing at the officer, who was still listening in, I told him I was talking on the only phone in the house.

"Then sit comfortably on the couch." He waited a second while I pretended to move from my station. "Now I want you to remove all your clothes. I want to teach you a few things that dirty old men like me expect." I couldn't believe what he was asking. My face turned bright red, knowing that the others were listening to him describe in detail what he wanted to do to me. Could he really see me? If so, then he'd know I was only pretending.

I didn't say much except an occasional "Okay" to let him know I had done as he asked. He was describing in detail every sex act he could think of. Most of the time I didn't listen to him and just came out with a few moans to let him think I was complying to his wishes.

After what seemed like an eternity, he stopped his fantasizing and said, "Get dressed. It's time we have our first real date! It's time to put into practice what you have learned. I would like to take some pictures of you for my collection."

This was it. I was finally going to meet my tormentor. He arranged to meet me at noon the following day in front of the bank two miles away.

"I know what you look like and will pick you up at twelve! Don't be late. Remember I know where you live and where your dad works!"

No sleep came that night. Would he show up? Would I be safe? At eleven the next day, Officer Corelli was at the door to go through the details. I was to meet the guy, get in his car, and continue going along with him. I was assured that an unmarked police car would always be behind me. Eleven forty-five came and we were off. The policeman drove me most of the way, letting me off two blocks from the planned meeting place. I walked the rest of the way slowly, feeling like I was walking my last steps on earth. I wanted to run the other way … cry…. But I walked on, knowing I could not back down now.

As I walked, I tried noticing the surroundings as if I would not see the familiar streets again. Stores were open for business as if it was any other ordinary day. Cars were passing by, their occupants busy with their daily chores. Kids were playing in their yards. Two boys were playing basketball at the nearby school. With every car that past, I was afraid it might be him.

I finally reached my destination, stopped and looked around. I didn't know who I was looking for. I had no description. Nothing. I saw the unmarked car a block away and breathed a sigh of relief. I noticed a few people enter the bank.

"Get in!" Suddenly there was a door opening next to me. I didn't even see him pull up. Suddenly, he was there in his bright red car. A big, stocky man reaching over the seat to open the door. I got in and felt like slamming that door behind me was the last link I had with anyone who could help. The man didn't talk. Just drove, heading to parts unknown. I used that time to look at last at the man behind the voice. He looked to be in his forties and unshaven, weighing over two hundred pounds. He was wearing overalls. I noticed a camera sitting on the seat between us. And … was that a gun within easy reach of his right hand?

I kept an eye on the mileage. One mile and soon two miles had past.

"How long do we have to go before the police show up? Are they still behind us?" Thoughts were running wild. I was afraid that the police had lost us along the way. What will happen when they do show up and the guy realizes he's been followed? Will he use his gun? After looking out the window, I realized we were heading away from town towards the woods. "Please make this nightmare end!" I screamed inside my thoughts. I felt the man's hand reach over and grab my thigh, squeezing till it hurt.

Sirens blared and I knew the end was almost here. Frantically the man looked out the window and saw the police trying to pull him over. "Damn! You told the cops! You'll be sorry!"

Suddenly there were police cars everywhere. For a few miles, he tried to outrun them. The speedometer reaching one hundred. He was swerving around cars that got in his way. I hung on; afraid it would end in a crash.

He was surrounded. Knowing there was no way out, he slowed down and pulled to the side of the road. Reaching for the gun, he grabbed me. Using me as a shield he forced me out of the car. The cold metal of the gun pushing into my neck, I felt paralyzed and closed my eyes. Waiting for the sound of the gun to go off. Inching away from the car, he dared the police to come closer.

Trembling and forcing back tears, I held my breath feeling that my short life was about to end. The police had the man surrounded.

"Let her go! There's no way out. Put down the gun!" I felt his hands relaxing and I could tell he knew it was hopeless. The gun left my neck and he backed away pushing me forward. I quickly ran as fast as I could into the closest policeman's arms. I was shaking but was glad it was over, and I was safe! I saw the man being handcuffed and led off to a waiting police car.

As I closed my eyes, I could almost see his face again. It was so long ago. I thought I had forgotten about that summer. Recalling it now made me realize that was just one of the many times when I needed my dad, but he was not there. Knowing what happened, he shrugged it off. He acted like he could care less that my life had almost ended. That he had no part in what happened that day, as if he wasn't the one who gave his permission to put my life in danger.

Later I would find out that the man who tried to take me that day was an Army buddy of my Dad's. He knew my mom had died, what times Dad was at work and that he had a young daughter who was home alone during the day. He knew exactly when I was home alone. He knew because Dad confided in his work friend in his time of grief unknowingly leading him to me.

Chapter 6

Along comes Gail

Winter 1959

The year was 1959. Mom had been gone for six months. I was paged to the principal's office during last period. They said Dad had been in a serious car accident. I left school and found my way to the hospital where I was told that he might not survive and was in critical condition. Dad looked so lifeless there in bed, hooked to machines to keep his body working. Was I to lose two parents in one year? Granted, Dad and I were barely speaking, but he was my father! There was nothing I could do for him. He was unconscious and didn't even know if I was there or not, so I didn't stay long. There were things to do at home, and people to notify about the accident.

I went home to an empty house. After calling Jackie to tell her what happened, I found Gail's phone number and started to dial. I didn't want to, but I knew Dad would want her to know. Gail was the woman he found that he had been corresponding with and according to Dad was the one he was serious about. It was the first time I had ever spoken to her. She reminded me of an Army sergeant barking orders, with no sympathy in her voice at all.

"Your dad needs me, so I'll get the first flight out. Tell him I am coming!" she insisted.

No matter what I said she would not take NO for an answer.

True to her word and wasting no time at all, Gail was at the front door within twenty-four hours, bags in hand, moving in like she owned the place. She not only talked like an Army sergeant, but she also acted and looked the part. All two hundred and fifty pounds of her!

Gail was short, just over 5 feet tall, round face and gold rim glasses stuck on the end of her nose.

Gail spent most days at the hospital, and I was at school, so we did not see much of each other those first few days. Dad pulled through miraculously and within a couple weeks he was sitting up in bed. He was in the hospital for at least four months. After a few weeks he was able to have weekend passes home. On December fifth, 1959, during one of his passes home, Dad and Gail were married in our front room with just the neighbors in attendance. It was now official. Gail was part of our family, like it or not!

My daily routine consisted of school, homework, cooking and housework. Yes, though Gail was part of the family, I still had to do all the things I did before she came! Suddenly Gail was sick. Too sick to take care of herself let alone take care of Dad and me. How she ever kept house in California I'll never know. Once again Dad had someone to take care of. When he wasn't there, I was nominated. And Gail ate it up. She loved getting as much out of me as she could.

I hated school but found myself spending more time there. I began helping the teachers and getting involved in after school activities or staying more at Bernice's house. Anything to stay away from home.

I remember clearly my first disagreement with Gail. It happened just one week after she married Dad, two weeks before Christmas. I was addressing Christmas cards to my relatives because I had always had that job. I did not yet consider Gail as family and neglected to include her name on the cards. After all, these cards were for Mom's family! All hell broke loose. She called me ungrateful and jealous, yelling at me! She tore up the cards one by one. Dad was still at the hospital and there was no one to turn to. He probably would have sided with her anyway. I knew then that life with Gail would be a kind of hell of its own. Boy was I right!

Chapter 7

My First Date

Summer 1961

American Lake, North Fort Lewis Washington. Eleven Miles from Tacoma. Twenty Minutes away by bus. It's where the soldiers go for a day of fun in the sun. Where families spend the day with their picnic baskets in their swimsuits and teenagers hung out with their friends.

It was a beautiful well-kept beach with lots of sand to run bare foot in. The lake's water was clear, perfect for swimming with ropes around a large area so you can't go too far out. Lifeguards sat on their high perches near the water's edge. On a clear day, you can see Mt. Rainier in the background. There was lots of green grass in the picnic area and food trucks set up ready to serve. On one side, there was a playground for the children and on the other, a tennis court. At night, the tennis court is changed into a dancing area with live music, where we can dance under the stars.

I would take the bus there every chance I got. At the lake, I felt free. Free of Dad and Gail. Free of the boys at school. And free of Nancy! The lake was a place where teenagers hung out and you could swim or just lay in the sand to sunbathe. And then there was dancing at night. There were many lonely soldiers, far away from home, welcoming any attention they could get. Ready to dance and party, no matter who they're with.

Bernice disapproved and told me so many times, trying to get me to stay away from the post. She stood by my side, never giving up on me. However, she would not go with me to the post, so I went alone.

One day, I met Jose. Better known by his American friends as Joe. He was Puerto Rican, and everything Dad was against, therefore very alluring to me. Joe was handsome, about 6 feet tall and weighed around 150 pounds. He had a dark tan, with black hair cut short in the back and sides and a little longer and wavy on top, and he seemed to notice me! I was lying on the grass watching the swimmers in the water. Soon he was next me, talking to me.

"What's a good-looking girl like you doing here all by yourself?" His accent was strong and sometimes hard to understand.

I couldn't believe he was talking to me! I loved his accent. Hearing him speak made my heart race.

"I bet you say that to all the girls you come across." I invited him to sit for a while. I didn't want him to leave and I just had to know more about the man behind that amazing voice.

I couldn't believe that was me, acting like that, talking to strangers. I was always shy and kept to myself. It was not like me to act this way but I kind of liked it. If Nancy could only see me now!

Joe and I talked for what seemed like hours. He talked about his country and how he missed home. He had been stationed at Fort Lewis for about six months and was still learning his way around. This was his first assignment as a soldier, having finished basic training a few months before.

"I might be taking my chances, considering we just met, but would you consider going out with me?"

This stranger was asking me out on what could possibly be my first date!

I knew I couldn't have him pick me up at home, so I lied to Dad and told him I was spending the night with Bernice. I met Joe at a local bowling alley. We bowled a few games and went out to eat. Innocent? It seemed so at the time. Joe didn't even make a pass at me. At the end of a wonderful evening, he dropped me off at Bernice's. Floating on air, I hated to see the night end.

I saw Joe as often as I could that week. After the second date, he started getting closer. Giving me my first kiss. First light, then heavy. I should have stopped him, but I enjoyed being kissed and the closeness we felt. I had the feeling that if I saw him again, there may be no turning back. I just knew that Joe cared for me. Maybe it could turn into something more.

Joe asked me out, not knowing at the time that it would be our last date. A night that would forever remain in my memory and give me nightmares for the rest of my life. A night, until now, no one knew about. Not even my best friend Bernice. A night I still blame myself for.

Joe asked me to meet him uptown for a late dinner. I took the city bus to downtown Tacoma and was let off on Pacific Avenue. I waited for what seemed like hours. It was dark, with only dim streetlights. There was nobody at the bus stop at that time of night. Suddenly, there appeared before me a strange man. I did not hear him approach so I was startled, becoming afraid of what could happen. All I could make out in the dark was a shadowy figure, touching me gently on the shoulder.

"Hi, I'm Luis, a friend of Jose's.", reaching his hand out to me. "Joe asked me to come here and bring you to him." Luis seemed like a giant in the dark, larger then Joe, his accent not as strong.

It didn't occur to me to ask why Joe hadn't come instead. I followed the man until I found myself at a run town hotel at the edge of town.

"Joe is visiting a friend here and couldn't get away. He asked that I take you to his room."

I wanted to see Joe and find out what was going on. Suddenly, the door swung open and Joe was there. He hugged me and apologized for not meeting me himself.

"I am so glad you could come." He said and instructed me to make myself comfortable. Luis then handed me a mixed drink.

I had never tasted liquor before and didn't like the taste. It was bitter, but I slowly sipped the drink anyway. I didn't know if it was the drink at the time, but I suddenly became very tired. My head was floating, and I felt like I was going to be sick. I wondered if this is what it felt like to be drunk, not suspecting that the way I was feeling could have been caused by anything else. Awake, I could hear voices around me, but they were just voices. I could not make out the words and I had no sense of time.

"How long have I been here?" I asked myself.

I felt Joe's arms around me and heard soft whispers in my ear but still couldn't understand what was being said. Or was it even Joe? At this point, I couldn't tell. But who else would be holding me like that? Suddenly, I felt my clothes being removed. I didn't have the strength to stop what was happening, but I tried to push him away with all my might anyway. At least I thought I was. I was just too weak to fight him off.

"Stop, please stop!" but did I yell it out or was my mind playing tricks on me? My head was in a cloud, struggling to make sense of what was happening.

I felt something hard being forced inside of me and I still couldn't find the strength to fight it. The pain was so unbearable. I could tell I was starting to bleed and began to cry but still, unable to make them stop. Them? Yes, there were more than one, or even two. I knew Joe was there, but I didn't recognize the other voices. I tried focusing and through blurry eyes, I could make out several faces, but I couldn't tell how many. They took turns repeatedly, laughing and talking in their language. I didn't understand their words, but I was glad I couldn't.

"Please God, let it be over!" I prayed.

My virginity was gone. At sixteen, it was something that I could never get back. This was a time I should enjoy being a kid. A time for parties and dances not that I was invited to many. I was trying to think of anything else but what was happening in the present.

Finally, it was over. I had no idea what time it was, but I knew it was early morning. The men were getting dressed, still drinking and laughing at my expense. Joe warned me not to mention that night to anyone. And I never did until now, within the words on these pages.

"You say anything, and you will live to regret it." and they were gone.

I slowly and painfully got myself dressed. All I wanted to do was leave that dirty hotel room. I was still bleeding. To this day, I don't remember how I had made it home in that condition. The night was such a blur. My thoughts were running rampant with things like: God, what if I'm pregnant? Should I tell someone? Who would believe me? I was warned to stay away from Joe. How can I face anyone? How and who could I tell? And Joes warning kept going through my head…"You say anything, you will live to regret it!"

I made my way home that morning and snuck into the house while Dad and Gail were still asleep, tiptoeing into the bathroom. All I wanted was a hot shower. My head ached and I still felt high from whatever it was that Joe slipped me. The bathroom was spinning, and I found myself leaning over the toilet to throw up. I swallowed two aspirins hoping the headache would go away. I needed to wash what had happened off me. I made the water as hot as I could stand and slowly stepped into the shower. I cried as I scrubbed in soap and water so hot it was turning my flesh red. I couldn't tell, unable to feel my body. Completely numb. I knew that I must go on with life and try to forget. I needed to be a better person and change. It's not too late.

"Just don't let me be pregnant!" I prayed.

To my relief, I started my period two weeks later. I never saw Joe again and I never spoke about what happened to anyone. I tried to forget that day so long ago but returning to the house brought everything back in a flood. I realized why it was always so hard for me to enter the bathroom in this house. As I stared at the shower, memories flew forward and I thought I could see the shadow of that lost little girl from long ago, behind the shower curtain. I could almost hear the hot, steamy water running and her sobbing once again.

Chapter 8

Truth about Jackie

Summer 1961

August 1961. That was when I learned the truth about my sister. They say it will come out eventually but the way I found out was unbearable. It wasn't Gail's place to tell me and how she did it, I will never forget.

Looking at my arm and hand, I can still see the scars, always reminding me of that day. The one on my eyebrow has faded to almost nothing but as I stare at my arm, I remember the cruelty in Gail's words. Why didn't Mom or Dad tell us years ago. Because of that day, I vowed that when I had children, I would always be honest with them.

On that day, I had an appointment to get my senior pictures taken for school. I was in the bathroom combing my hair and putting on my makeup. I was to meet Bernice in an hour at the bus stop on the corner. We were about to become seniors and looking forward to having our pictures taken.

Gail was sitting on the couch, drinking her coffee. The front room was just off the bathroom by a few feet. When the door was open, the couch could be seen from the bathroom sink. She didn't waste any time to start in on me, "You didn't do the dishes, you idiot." I was used to her verbal abuse by now.

"I don't know why you're even bothering with that make-up. Sure doesn't do you any good!"

I stopped and glared at her, saying nothing. Comments like that weren't new to me. I just learned to ignore them.

"You're just like your mother. A tramp!" She continued.

I don't know what set her off that day. I wasn't talking to her and she had no reason to start in on her attacks. This time, her comments got to me because she brought Mom into it.

"At least I'm not a fat cow like you!" I spat back.

No one talks about my mother that way. Gail didn't even know her.

"My mother was twice the woman you are! How dare you say anything bad about her!" I yelled.

"Ha!" was her reply. "From what I'm told your mom was a whore! And your sister is proof of that!"

What was she talking about? Mom and Dad were married long before Jackie was born. There were stories of us as children. Certainly, they would have told us instead of keeping something like that a secret. Besides, if that was true, how would Gail know?

To this day I can't recall everything that was said. I just remember screaming at her.

"You're lying!"

I lunged towards her, wanting to take out my frustration and anger. She was the last person who should cast stones! When I reached out for her, she dropped the cup she was holding which fell and broke into many pieces.

Gail picked up a piece of glass and started swinging it, calling me names and saying that she wanted me out of the house. She kept striking me with the glass in her hand. With each swing, I felt a stinging pain. I was so angry. I didn't notice at first the blood that was dripping down my arm and on my face.

"You are the one who should leave! I hate you!" Tears rolled down my face.

My arm, eyebrow and cheek were cut. The blood was everywhere. It would have been worse but a policeman showed up at our front door. I don't know who called them, but I assumed it was the neighbor. They broke us up and called an ambulance.

I got fifty-two stitches which left scars that remained for the rest of my life, reminding me of that day. I stayed in the hospital for two days, miserable and alone with a lot of time to think.

I never understood why the police asked Gail if she wanted to press charges since she was the one who started it. Again, Dad sided with Gail! He never came to visit me those two days. He only came to the hospital to take me home. During the ride, Dad explained that he was disappointed in me and I was to get along with Gail, doing whatever she says, or he would send me to another home to live. He then proceeded to tell me what Gail had so cruelly blurted out.

"I married your mom in 1943, one year before you were born, Jackie was six at the time." He almost whispered the words

"Your mom was very young, in love with a married man and had his child. Jackie never knew, and I want it to remain that way. We decided to raise her as my own and give her my name."

As I stared at the wounds on my arm. I wanted to tell Jackie the truth, but I knew it wasn't my place and I would be in trouble if I did.

It would be decades later and soon after Dad was gone before I would tell her what I had learned on that fateful day.

Chapter 9

Lloyd

1961- 1962

I couldn't wait to be a senior. All I ever dreamed about was being able to leave home, Dad, and especially Gail to start a new life. I didn't care what kind of life that was, but anything would be better than the life I had at home.

I was seventeen, a senior at last! Only a short time left until I could rid myself of the pain that was this house. Not a day went by that I didn't think of running away from home. Having no place to go and no money kept me from going through with it. Also having that diploma would open doors. I could get a job and find a place of my own. This dream is what kept me going.

Nobody at school had questioned the scars on my face. Even as a senior I was still a "nothing", not worthy of notice. I continued to get involved in after school activities so I would not have to go home. A part of me had hoped that I could gain some friends by being in these clubs but again I was ignored. They acted as though I wasn't even there but that was still better than being at home.

I was at Bernice's house one day in October when a guy I had never seen before popped in for a visit.

"Barbara, I'd like you to meet my cousin Lloyd".

Lloyd was not a handsome guy, just average. He reminded me of Fonzie on Happy Days. He wore a black leather jacket, was rough around the edges, black wavy hair, and kept his hands in his pockets. Lloyd's father was married to Bernice's aunt, though he did not live with the two. I later found out he lived in a foster home close by. I understood why Bernice never spoke of him before. Lloyd was into everything. Drugs, alcohol, theft, you name it. He had spent half his life in juvenile homes, just turned eighteen and he noticed me!

"HI Barbara, I've heard a lot about you. I'm glad we finally got to meet."

I had this feeling that I should run. The way he was dressed and the way he talked gave me the feeling he was bad news. Having dealt with guys like Lloyd in the past, I should have run... run far way but he was Bernice's cousin, I should at least give him a chance.

"I wish I could say the same. I haven't seen you around here before."

Lloyd smiled that crooked smile, with hands still in his pockets

"I've been pretty busy, but I get to this neck of the woods occasionally." He said

The bells went off in my head. The warnings were screaming at me. I should have left but Instead I jumped into another situation that I helped create.

Lloyd asked me out on a date that night and I accepted.

"Would you like to go to a movie with me tonight. It's a good movie and I'd hate to see it alone?"

Again, I did not listen to Bernice's warnings.

"He's my cousin. I know better than anybody that he's trouble. Please don't go."

I should have listened!

Lloyd picked me up at my house that night. I couldn't care less if Dad or Gail disapproved! By then I was used to doing things against their wishes. The more they said no, the more I did it.

We saw a movie and then went for a ride out of town to a parking place popular to teenagers. It was a beautiful night and I didn't want it to end, though I knew what would happen once we parked.

Lloyd wasted no time. He started kissing me and I didn't resist. Someone was showing me love, but no one ever told me about protection. I thought since that one horrific night with Joe and his friends didn't leave me pregnant, then one time with Lloyd should be safe.

Sex with Lloyd was so different but remembering the rape caused me to tighten up, which made it hard to relax. Lloyd went slow, trying to please me, but all I could see was Joe's face. I wished it was over and felt relief when it was. It seemed to last for hours. I was disappointed that I didn't feel any of the excitement that was supposed to be there. I only hoped Lloyd could not tell I was pretending. If having someone to love me meant I had to submit to sex to get that love, then I could pretend, and he would never know.

Lloyd was quiet afterward. He sat as far away from me as he could staring out the window. After a few minutes Lloyd said, "I guess I should get you home."

I didn't care if I only knew Lloyd for one day, or if I ever see him again. All I cared about was the present time and someone was holding me and loving me. I knew it had to end and I would have to go home, to reality.

Lloyd didn't call me after that night, it was obvious he was only after one thing. I wondered if he knew that I didn't enjoy the sex as much as I pretended. The sex I so freely gave.

Christmas came and went like all the others. The only thing I was grateful for was that the year was ending. One more bad year to put behind me and another step closer to being eighteen. Closer to being free of my current life. Little did I know that time was just around the corner, not waiting for my eighteenth birthday as I had thought. I was closer to being free than I realized.

Entering a new year should have been a new start. At seventeen I was one of the youngest in my senior class. Most of the class was planning for their senior prom and graduation. It should have been a time for me to party and have fun. It was the last link to my childhood before facing the responsibilities of adulthood. It should have been, but with the missing of my period, adulthood came earlier than planned. I was pregnant!

I missed a period in December, but it did not dawn on me until I also missed one in January. I didn't need a doctor to tell me what I already knew. I wasn't ready to be a mother. I could hardly manage my own life without taking on the responsibility of another one.

"What was I going to do? How was I going to tell dad?"

I wanted to be out of the house and on my own. Now I have a way. Maybe the love I was seeking since Mom died would finally come in the form of a baby. I child of my own that would love me unconditionally.

I needed to tell Lloyd first, he had a right to know. Life with him had to be better than the one I was living now. That is if he wanted to have a life with me. I was not sure if Lloyd would do the right thing, but he had to! I needed him to. With trembling hands, I picked up the phone to call him.

"Hello Lloyd, its Barbara. I need to see you right away."

He did not bat an eye when I told him.

"I'm pregnant. I'm really scared! What are we going to do?"

Lloyd surprised me by insisting on coming with me to confront Dad. Afterall, I hadn't heard from him in a couple months. I didn't think he would care and insist it was my problem.

"It's going to be ok Barbara. Let's go see your dad together."

I think for both of us, it was a chance to get out of our present home situations and a chance to be adults.

Why was I so scared to tell Dad? He never cared about what happened to me before! As far as I knew, he would be glad to get rid of me.

That's exactly how he felt. "You made your bed now lie in it," as the saying goes, fit perfectly, word for word.

He didn't have to say anything when we told him. His expression said it all.

I could read my dad's mind like a book. He did not seem surprised or concerned about me, only about, "What the neighbors will say?"

I had to leave school, not that I would miss it, but I would miss being with Bernice and I would miss graduation.

Chapter 10

Here comes the Bride

February 1962

After very little thought, Dad and Gail decided we would get married in Idaho. We were not asked but told what we were going to do.

Some parents would forgive your mistakes and open their arms to you. Not mine. I was a disgrace to not only them, but their friends in the church.

Washington state would require Lloyd to have parental consent. As much as I wanted Bernice to be with me, I had no choice. I was ordered to pack my bag and prepare for the long trip to Coeur D'alene Idaho. I still had to have a guardian along and Gail was elected! Dad refused to participate.

It was a long drive to Idaho in Lloyd's old beat up old car. We didn't know if we'd make it out of town, let alone across the state. Several times we stopped to let the car cool down. It overheated, ran dry of oil, the tire went flat, but we kept going, praying all the way.

Gail sat in the back seat, behind me, saying nothing during the entire trip. I felt her glare on me, heard her breathing and occasional cough, but otherwise, she remained quiet.

We reached our destination, twelve hours later! Coeur d'Alene Idaho, just over the Washington border, a few miles from Spokane. Where I was to be married and dumped off with a man I hardly new. Where I would start my new life. A life of uncertainty.

I was a young nervous bride, about to enter a new life with a man I didn't love. I wanted to run, hide, hitch-hike back into time, but I sat next to Lloyd whom I barely knew. Gail sat behind me leaving me wishing I didn't know her at all and that she would just go away. I wanted to cry but didn't want either of them see me give in to tears. I endured the long ride in silence.

We found a cheap, run down hotel and paid for two rooms for the night. I washed up and combed my hair while Lloyd checked a phone book for a place to get married.

Within an hour, we were standing in the doorway of a nearby Justice of the Peace. It was nine in the evening and the old man looked like he wanted to be there about as much as I did.

This was not the wedding I had always dreamed of, with a beautiful white gown, walking down the aisle to the man of my dreams, and riding off into the sunset in a horse drawn carriage.

This wedding reminded me of an episode of the Andy Griffith show that I remembered. In it, Andy was in a night shirt and hat, marrying these two, with shot gun in hand. There was no shot gun, but there was a vision of Andy, complete with his night cap, and his wife, a spitting image of Aunt Bea. Instead of a shot gun there was Gail, arms folded, standing there like a sergeant in the army, making sure the participants would not escape. I tried my best not to burst out laughing at the sight. I have to say this comical vision was the only highlight of the trip.

On February fourteen, 1962, Valentine's day, a day for lovers, I was married in less than twenty minutes. Without my mom or best friend. While the kids at school were planning their proms, I was planning for my new married life. "Till death do us part."

That sentence scared me. I was only seventeen! Death seemed a long way off to live with someone you didn't love, and who I was sure didn't love me.

After the ceremony, the three of us went to have supper and then headed back to our rooms. Another moment I dreaded. I never did like sex. Rape does that to you. I only thought of having sex as a way to be close to someone, to get the love I craved. Now I was faced with having to submit to it because it was the duty of a wife.

Lloyd was gentle and I can't blame him if I didn't enjoy it. I pretended, something I became good at. After he was satisfied, or so I hoped, Lloyd rolled over and went to sleep. I didn't sleep that night. I cried silently and wondered why things happen to me the way they did.

"Was I really the bad person Dad always said I was? What would happen to me from now on?"

I rubbed my tummy and silently assured my baby that things would be all right.

Lloyd had a job waiting for him as a farmhand in Washington, about thirty miles from Idaho. The next morning, we drove Gail to the airport, and we headed to the farm.

The town was in nowhere land! It reminded me somewhat of Jolon, no other town in sight and no neighbors! The only two humans around were the man and woman who owned the farm. There was no one for me to talk to but the man's wife who was at least sixty years old. There was no television, no radio, nothing for me to do but work, from morning to night. I was not eighteen yet and even though I was pregnant, I was expected to clean all day for my hungry, dirty husband.

Lloyd changed from the carefree teenager to a demanding husband. He was busy on the farm and was tired and short tempered with me when he came home at night. He didn't see to my needs, never having any time to show me attention.

Every little thing I did seemed to be wrong. The house wasn't clean enough, the choices I made for dinner were never the right ones, and I was never allowed to have any sicknesses that went along with being pregnant.

I longed for my chats with Bernice. I didn't entirely blame Lloyd. He had no idea what marriage was supposed to be like. He never had a family life and at the foster homes he was in, he was led to believe that the woman had a place in life. To work and take care of their man.

Two months was all I could take. I was not old enough or experienced enough to handle even the smallest problems and so I took the easy way out. I ran! I talked the lady of the farm into taking me to a nearby town to do some shopping. I stuffed what I could in my purse, took what money I could find, wrote Lloyd a short note, and I left.

"Dear Lloyd. I am sorry. I feel we were both pushed into something we were not ready for. A baby cannot bring us happiness for long. You need to go on with your life. I need my life back."

It was easier once in town to slip away. I bought a bus ticket for Portland. Before I knew it, I was on my way to my mom's family. My aunts and cousins lived there. People I knew would help me and love me.

It was about a twenty-hour bus ride. A trip I recall vaguely. I slept some, but mostly I looked out the window at the passing scenery and wondered how I had gotten into this mess. It seemed like every step I took forward; I went back five. I yearned for that little girl again from so long ago. I wanted my mother's arms around me, to have her dry my tears. To assure me that she would make things better.

The marriage had ended, and I had no idea where I was headed but I tried not to look back. I reached for a handkerchief to dry my eyes and saw the wedding ring on my finger. A ring that should have never been there to begin with. I found myself slipping it off my finger and dropping it to the floor of the moving bus.

Chapter 11

Rosemont Home for Girls

1962

Nobody expected me. I didn't even know where I was going until I found myself on the bus heading south. I took everyone by surprise when I showed up, with only the clothes on my back, at my cousin Pat's front door.

Pat had blond hair, medium length. She stood about five foot seven, just a little taller than I was. She always wore glasses and liked her beer cold.

"Why Barbara, this is a surprise."

I just knew I could seek help and shelter from her. I knew she would understand, and I was right. I was welcomed with open arms.

"I just needed to leave. I couldn't take living with Lloyd anymore and I couldn't go home to Dad. I have nowhere to go." I promised myself I'd be strong, but just then, the tears started to fall.

There were no questions asked. Pat hugged and welcomed me with open arms. I was soon bedded down in a room shared with three of Pat's kids. I was with Mom's family, knowing everything would be ok. By then, I was four months pregnant, still feeling the effects of nausea and starting to show. I couldn't work and I didn't know how long I could expect free room and board with Pat. She barely made ends meet supporting her own kids as it was.

My Aunt Stella and Uncle Lewis drove the long distance to Lloyd's and the farm to get my belongings. I had no clothes and no money to buy any, so I needed my things. Lloyd gave them my clothes reluctantly after a few choice words from my uncle but refused to give them the one thing that meant the most to me. A colored portrait of Mom. It was lost to me forever when he decided to keep it.

I was only at Pat's for two weeks when we both decided I had to make other arrangements.

The added burden was a big strain on Pat. She loved me but I could not expect her to take care of me. Where would I go? Dad would not have me back. Returning to Lloyd was out of the question.

Aunt Vi and Aunt Mae did some research and found a home in Portland for girls who were in the same situation as me. I didn't want to go but how could I refuse? I agreed to check it out.

In May I reluctantly made the move to my new home. I wanted to cry but what good would it do. Again, I felt unwanted, a burden to everyone around me. I was afraid of the future for me and my baby.

Rosemont, a school and treatment facility for troubled teens, was just another place where I didn't belong. Rosemont was primarily a home for Juvenile girls, Girls who constantly got in trouble, either at home, with the law, or at school. They were the incorrigibles, I was the minority, I was married, pregnant and never in trouble. I didn't belong there, but I had no choice.

Rosemont consisted of three buildings. The first building, Teen Haven One, was a small house unlike the other two. It appeared like a house anyone would live in. It was a one-story rambler with a kitchen, bathroom, four bedrooms, living room with a television, and a bookcase loaded with lots of books that any teenager would enjoy reading. Just a place to get together, hang out or enjoy a good book. In the front of the house was a reception desk and a small office to interview prospective clients and their families, or to talk privately with the girls already living there. It usually housed no more than eight girls. We were required to stay there for two weeks while we underwent a physical, counseling, and to learn the rules of the house, one of which was to never go outside. During those two weeks of isolation I had very little contact with the other residents. I'd see them come and go and we'd say hi in passing, but we preferred to be alone with our thoughts. Soon I would find out what it was like at the big house and what kind of girls lived there, because before I knew it, my time would be up, and I will be shipped off a few yards away to live amongst them.

The one good thing I remembered about Teen Haven One, was the house mother Hildegard, (Hilde for short). Hilde did the cooking, cleaning, hand holding, listening, drying tears and lots of hugs. She seemed to care about us and our futures. Hilde was short, just over five feet tall, round figure, in her sixties with graying hair. She reminded me a lot of my mother. I hated that we could only be with Hilde for two weeks, but the time came when I had to move to the big house.

Teen Haven Two was a short walk up an incline. The house was two stories and bigger than any house I have ever seen. There was a large cafeteria where we ate all our meals, an office, large front room which included a library, television area, work area that held a desk to do our studies, and large bay windows that we could look out to see the beautiful gardens. There were six bedrooms upstairs and two bathrooms. Each bedroom could hold four girls.

The workers there consisted of a cook and her assistant, a cleaning lady, and a housemother, Janet, who was nothing like Hilde. Janet was all business. Wire rim glasses, reddish hair held in a bun, skinny and very tall.

We followed the rules if we didn't want the punishment given out by Janet. Whether it was confinement to our rooms, extra homework, help in the kitchen or whatever she could think of to make our lives more miserable. "Because I told you so!" was her favorite phrase.

And then there was Gary. The only man that worked at the facility. He was the counselor and the one that made the decision to let you go home, stay at Rosemont or be moved to a more structured environment. He was all business with his neatly pressed suits, shined shoes, handlebar moustache, and somewhere in his mid-fifties. Gary came once a week, occupying the office and spoke to each of us privately.

"Hi, I'm Gary" holding out his hand to me. "How is your stay here so far?"

"Okay, I guess." I took his hand shyly wishing I was anywhere but in his office.

The one advantage of moving to the big house was I could finally go outside. The property was large with a perfect green lawn, walkways to stroll around in, beautiful gardens full of flowers, scattered picnic tables, and benches to sit and take in the fresh air. The whole property was surrounded by a high wooden fence, so we couldn't see out and no one could see in.

Weather permitting, I spent a lot of time outside, sitting on a bench, getting lost in a book and pretending I was the character I'd read about.

A short walk behind the house was our school. It held four classrooms and a teacher lounge. The teachers taught more than one subject. We were able to transfer our credits from whatever public school we came from.

The girls at Rosemont ranged in ages from fifteen to eighteen. During the time of my stay there, the girls who were there the longest were the ones who were in charge. You didn't dare double-cross them or make them angry in any way. These particular girls were from broken homes, in detox from their drug habits and who came in out of detention centers often.

I was in the minority group of girls which consisted of only me. The one married, pregnant girl there. I didn't fit into any group and once again I found myself being different from everybody else. I felt like I was back in high school and standing alone against the world, this time without Bernice by my side. A journey I must take alone.

I saw Gary weekly. His job was to guide me in any future decision I would make after leaving Rosemont. During my sessions with Gary, I quickly learned that the plan they had for me was to leave here with I bright future ahead of me and a fresh start...without my baby!

"It's the best thing for you and your baby." Gary said repeatedly. "How can you take care of a baby at your age with no education or job training?"

How did he know what was best for me or my baby? I will finally have someone to love me unconditionally. I would find a way to make a life for my baby even if I must do it alone. Nobody is taking this child away from me! But how was I going to make it happen?

Gary was against teenagers becoming mothers. I never would have come here had I known this. The possibility of anyone trying to take my baby away from me had never crossed my mind. With each session I felt the pressure to give up my baby.

"I've contacted social services. They will be here next week to tell you your options." Gary said

This baby would finally be something that is a part of me. Mine to love and who would love me in return. I knew keeping the baby would be difficult. I had no job training and nowhere to live but I had to try to make it work. I didn't even have a high school diploma. The baby was due in September. Time was passing by and I knew I had decisions to make and soon. Decisions that would affect the rest of my life.

One thing I did know is that I wouldn't be talking to social services. Not now, not ever! When they come, I'd listen with closed ears? I had no choice. They made the choice for me. But till my baby was here, the decision would be mine and mine alone. Also, I was married. That should account for something!

I did not expect this woman, Margie, from social services to arrive with forms in hand, ready for me to sign my baby away that very day.

"It's for the best Barbara, we will find a good home for your baby." She said, echoing the same words as Gary in my previous meetings with him.

How could they promise that?

"You don't know that. It's my baby! Mine for life!" I tore up the papers, threw them at her and ran from the room.

The only two things I liked about that house were being able to be outside as much as I wanted and going to school, even though we were required to attend. I never thought I'd enjoy studying or homework. It gave me something to do and a way to forget my problems for a while. I only needed a few credits and was determined to get my diploma.

June was graduation. The only good thing that came out of my stay at Rosemont. The ceremony was nice with cap and gown. Some of the girls even had their families in attendance. Pat skipped work that day and came to see me graduate, but no one else came. Probably because I told no one else. I knew my aunts would have been there, but I did not want to burden them anymore then I had.

I received my diploma, which the school was able to obtain from my High School, Franklin Pierce. I convinced myself that little piece of paper would be my way out.

I still had over two months after graduation before my baby was due. Without school, I had more time to think. More time to plan on what to do with the rest of my life. More time to deal with the other residents of Teen Haven Two.

Mary was one of those residents I was learning to tolerate. She had wavy black hair that reached just above her shoulders and was average height and weight. She had olive skinned with dark brown eyes almost...black. Her eyes seemed to spark with fury. She spit her hateful words through clenched teeth.

"Hey there, you're in my space!" She said as she pushed me out of the way.

"Sorry." I mumbled as a moved away from her.

"Do you hear that girls? She's sorry. Fatso's sorry"

Being near her reminded me of Nancy back at Franklin Pierce High School. Mary was one of those girls you didn't cross. The other girls tended to do exactly as they were told. Strangely, I remember Mary's name, but I not the names of the girls who were nice to me. She taunted and teased me, asking how any man would want to get close enough to me to get me pregnant. She seemed to always try to get me alone making me fearful of her and what she might do.

Mary was a lesbian and made sure everyone knew it. She was always trying to hit on the new girls, hoping to score with any one of them. I tried to stay clear of her as much as I could. Sometimes it was impossible to stay out of her way.

It was always when I was in the shower that Mary happened to be as well. She seemed to watch me, trying to catch me alone, naked, either getting in or out of the shower. The showers were away from the main living area, upstairs in the back of the house, were no one can hear you. Mary took advantage of the quiet to do as she pleased whenever she wanted.

"Well look whose here. All nice and naked." The tone in her voice was flat with no emotion.

I grabbed a towel to cover myself. "Leave me alone." I told her

"I'll leave you alone if that's what you really want." She reached for me and yanked the towel away.

I started to scream as Mary shoved her hand over my mouth.

"You tell anyone about what happens here, and you will live to regret it." She forced her mouth on mine and squeezed my breast.

"I always wondered what it'd be like to make love to someone who's with child." She said.

"Please. I won't tell. Just leave me alone." I cried out as she slipped her fingers inside me. "Please, my baby"

After a few long minutes. Mary left and I was alone, kneeling to the floor, crying and hurting, vowing to never be alone with her again. After that day I made sure I was never alone in the bathroom. Never to take a shower again, but sponge bathed at the sink. Never allowing myself to be caught naked again as long as I lived there.

August came and I was eight months along, feeling very uncomfortable and unsure of what the weeks ahead would bring. The further along I was, the more pressure was put on me to give up my baby. The papers that would sign my baby away were always within reach. I knew if I were to keep the baby with me, I had to leave before I gave birth.

On one of Pat's visits, I decided to confide in her. I told her everything, from the pressure to give my baby away to the treatment of the other girls. I even told her what Mary did to me that day in the shower. Together we schemed to get me out of there.

It was easy to put myself in the home, it should have been easy getting me out. They would not let me walk out freely. I was still underage and considered by now a ward of the court even though I was married. There was not much time left because the baby was due in two weeks, and so we planned… "The great Escape.

Chapter 12

It's a Boy

1962

September first. That would be the day I walked,
no, ran from that place, not knowing where I was running
to. I knew things would fall into place and I would be okay.
I just hoped things went as planned and that I didn't get
caught leaving. I started to panic as the day drew closer
and now it was here. At two in the morning, I was packed.
I didn't have much to take with me. What I did have fit into
my pillowcase. At least in the big house there were no
locks, so I could easily slip out the door. I soon found
myself in the yard and running, wanting to look back to see
if I was being followed. It wasn't far to the fence and that
was my only obstacle.

I was nine months pregnant and faced with
climbing the fence to freedom. I was afraid that maybe Pat
wouldn't come as she promised, but she was there,
whispering my name, urging me on.

"Barbara, here I am. The fence isn't that tall. You
can do it"

I managed to climb over with her help. Pat was
there, but I almost didn't recognize her.

Dressed in farmer overalls, with a straw hat, and
sunglasses, the whole scene was rather comical. Since it
was dark, she looked out of place, especially with the
shades.

"I didn't want anyone to recognize me." She
shrugged and looked around to see if she was followed.

After a short hug, we were in her car and I was free! I kept looking back to see if anyone followed us, expecting to hear police sirens, but it was quiet. We didn't speak for a while. Our minds were on getting away, but eventually Pat broke the silence.

"Are you okay?"

"I think so." Now that we were far away, I started to cry.

"I have a place for you to go for a few days until they stop looking for you." Pat said. "A school friend of mine said they will put you up for a while."

I was grateful for her help and to be free of that place but now, all I could think of was going somewhere else for me to be where I don't belong. Someone else to have to take care of me.

Twenty minutes later, Pat parked the car in front of a small house on the outskirts of town. I don't remember too much about my stay there.

Cindy was Pats age and from what I was told, was a school friend. She was short, about five feet tall. Her long wavy hair flowed around her shoulders as she was flipping it out of her eyes while she was introduced to me, whispering so as not to wake up her husband.

"Hi Barbara. Pat has told me a little about your situation. Welcome to my home."

Cindy was a gracious host. She made me comfortable and left me alone to think which I did a lot of in the three weeks I stayed with her. I still didn't know what I was going to do once the baby was born. I could hardly take care of myself. I knew the baby would have the love I hadn't had for a long time.

Evidently the home didn't want me either. As far as I knew they didn't try to come and find me. They had Pat's address and we thought they would contact her. Pat just knew the police would be knocking on her door, but no one ever came to inquire about me.

I thought my due date was sometime around September tenth. That day came and went without my going into labor. Pat and I decided I would stay with Cindy until the baby was born if she would have me. Thankfully, she still welcomed me into her home. As the days passed, I grew anxious, scared of giving birth. I was not told what to expect. I was about to give birth and didn't feel I was ready. I didn't have any clothes, crib, or anything a baby would need. And when I moved so often, I would not be able to carry much with me.

The evening of September twenty-seventh I started going into labor. It was a pain I never knew before. I felt like I was going to die.

Cindy was watching television when I came to her. We timed the pains for a while to make sure, and then called Pat. We planned to meet her at the hospital. At least I would not be alone. To this day I owe Pat a lot for being there with me and for holding my hand when I needed it.

Labor seemed to last forever. It was painful and very exhausting, but I was determined for once to do something right. Eight hours later, in the wee hours of the morning, on September twenty-eight, it was over. I gave birth to a beautiful nine-pound baby boy. As I cuddled my son in my arms for the first time, I vowed to take care of him and love him forever. I was thankful that I did not give up my son. Together we would conquer any problems ahead. I named my son Bradley Scott. I heard once that Mom had planned to give me that name if I had been a boy. It was her favorite name, so I thought it was fitting. In honor of her, Brad was born.

I was in the hospital for three days, time to think and plan for our future. As much as Pat has helped me, I knew that living with her was not a permanent solution. I missed Tacoma and Bernice and knew I would return as soon as I could. I didn't hear from Bernice as much as I would have liked during the time I was in Portland. She had her own problems and neither one of us was good at writing letters. I knew I would see her sometime soon.

By the time Brad was born, Dad was overseas in Korea. I rarely heard from him and never heard from Gail. I wanted to tell him about Brad but did not know how to reach him, and I refused to contact Gail. I also felt Lloyd should know he had a son, so I wrote to the last address I had for him. I hoped he had gotten the letter, but he never responded.

Pat picked me up the day I was released from the hospital. Together, Brad and I went with her to our temporary home. As much as I had to deal with and as much pain as I had in the past, I now had one thing that I haven't had since Mom's death. I now had someone who loved me and trusted me with his life, my son.

"I will never let you down, sweet Brad. We will move on and things will only get better." I promised.

I stayed with Pat for three weeks. I wanted to be on my own, but I found the responsibilities of a baby tiring. I also had to look after Pat's four kids to earn my keep. She understood why I wanted to leave and bought me a ticket to Tacoma. I appreciated all she did for me, and she will always have a special place in my heart.

All I could think of was going home, but what would happen when we got there? I had no money, no job, and a baby to take care of. I couldn't even nurse Brad. The doctors said that I didn't have an ample enough milk supply to nourish him, so I had to find a way to get formula, and that took money.

The bus ride took three hours. Brad slept most of the way. What would I do when I get there? Would Gail help me? Probably not! And Dad was still away. As soon as I got off the bus, I called Bernice, but there was no answer. What was I going to do next? I couldn't stay at the bus depot forever.

I started walking, carrying Brad, lost and alone once again, eventually finding myself in front of the Salvation Army. They're supposed to be there for people in need, I sure qualified for that! From the ads I've seen, all you had to do was ask.

I entered their door with Brad in my arms, and tears in my eyes.

"Can you help?" I asked to anyone who would listen.

I practically begged for some shelter for the night, some food, anything. It was Friday, the time was one in the afternoon. Apparently, their lunch hour.

"Come back later." Everyone's gone to lunch. The woman behind the counter told me.

I sat outside and waited for the workers to return. Two o'clock came. Everyone returned along with a line of other people pushing their way to the front of the line. I tried to get their attention. I was told that they were busy and asked me to wait, yet again.

"No one is able to help you at this moment. Have a seat. We'll call you as soon as we can"

Brad was getting fussy and hungry. He needed a diaper change, but I waited. They had to call me soon!

Four o'clock came and they were starting to close.

"I'm sorry we can't help you today. Come back Monday!", was their response.

That was more important to them than helping me. They could see I was holding a baby. They knew I'd been waiting there all day! It was closing time and they couldn't be bothered. All they cared about was getting off work and getting home to their families early since it was Friday.

I vowed from that day forward I would not ever ask the Salvation Army for help, and to never set foot in their doors again.

"What was I going to do between Friday and Monday?" I had to get something to feed Brad and I couldn't let him sleep on the streets while we just wait for someone to help.

I walked some more, most of the time in circles, trying to find a place for the night. Brad was fussy and wet. I passed a bench, changed him, and fed him the last of the formula. I finally stopped at a phone and called Gail. I was desperate and willing to crawl back to her for mercy. If she would only get me some formula for the baby. But she laughed

"You made your bed..."

The same thing she had said to me since she entered my life. I hung up on her in mid-sentence.

I continued walking. The sun was starting to sink, and I was getting scared. What would happen when the darkness arrived? Somehow, I found myself in front of the offices for the Goodwill. They were less known for giving a helping hand, but I had to try. I didn't have to say anything when I entered their door. The receptionist took one look at me and took charge.

"Oh dear, let me have the baby and you sit. I'll get you a cup of cocoa."

Rachel looked to be in her sixties, with a round face, glasses sitting on the edge of her nose. She looked to weigh about one hundred and seventy pounds. Her smile was big and for the first time that day, I felt relaxed.

With just a few phone calls she found emergency housing, and one month's rent paid. I had no furniture, dishes or bedding, but at last I had a roof over my head. Since it was Friday Night, I could not do much. Every place was closed, but Rachel promised to come back Monday to take me to the welfare office. She stopped at the store and picked up formula for Brad and some food and necessities for me to get by until Monday.

That weekend has never been forgotten. I sat huddled in a corner, holding my baby, cuddling him in my coat as it was cold and I had no blankets, singing to my Brad, promising him a better future. His life started out badly, but I was determined that his future would be brighter.

On Monday, as she promised, Rachel was at the door. She drove me to the welfare office and helped me filled out the forms. I was given emergency money and a voucher for food. After we finished Rachel stopped at the Goodwill with more vouchers and let me pick out many things I would need. It was like Christmas to me. I selected blankets, baby clothes, some clothes for me and a few dishes to get by. Again, I found myself in someone's debt. Rachel will always be remembered. The Goodwill will always have my support.

I started making a mental note of all those in my life that I would someday thank, but words will never be enough. Maybe those mentioned will recognize themselves in this story and know how much I appreciated their help and how I may not have survived without it. Maybe the ones who refused to lend a hand will recognize themselves as well. I hold no grudges. I did at the time, but time for revenge has passed. If they can see how they let one lonely seventeen-year-old down years ago, when all she wanted was a helping hand or a kind word, maybe they will learn as I have and reach out for the next girl who cries out for help.

I stayed in the house for the remainder of the year. It was close to Christmas and I knew it would be hard to make a move at that time. The money that welfare gave me just barely covered the rent and electricity. I washed our clothes in the bathtub and lived on cheese and beans. Brad's formula consisted of watered-down powdered milk, but despite it all, he was gaining and thriving.

I was finally able to get in touch with Bernice and she visited often. She offered to let me stay with her and help with the housework. This would allow me to eventually get a job to help. That sounded like heaven to me. I would be living with my best friend. I would have someone to talk to and confide in, like old times. And Brad would have two moms to spoil him. She had a job as a dishwasher in a nursing home and a small apartment. Bernice's wages were enough to pay her rent and necessities and with what I received from welfare, we managed to get by. I received what we called in those days "commodities" which would later be replaced by food stamps. Commodities consisted of flour, sugar, peanut butter, rice, shortening and powdered milk. We became quite experienced in creating meals using what we had. One of the things we made quite often was what we liked to call "Paste Cakes" consisting of nothing but the flour and water mixed together and fried with the shortening. Brad thrived on the powdered milk, we thrived on Paste Cakes.

That Christmas was a lonely one. At least I had Bernice and Brad. There was not much money for a tree or gifts but luckily Brad was too young to know the difference and I vowed to make it up to him. Some day. Another year gone; another year remembered. Another year that could be forgotten. If only I could.

Chapter 13

Britton Trip

Summer 1963

The end of 1962 was approaching. I had hoped things would be better once I moved in with Bernice, but one thing I learned was never to move in with your best friend, if you want to remain best friends. We had clashing personalities, and seldom agreed on anything. Bernice worked all day and was tired and grumpy when she got home. I didn't keep the house clean enough or cook the right meals and the baby's crying got to her. She felt I wasn't doing my share to help with the finances, and she was right. In order to keep our friendship, I knew I had to move out.

After three months, I moved into my own apartment. Things were the same at the end of last year as they had been in the beginning. I was alone, struggling to make ends meet. Brad was growing and was now ten months old. Every day, when he would hug me, I knew, no matter how hard it got, I would never regret my decision to keep my son.

I needed a change. I wanted out of Tacoma, even if only for a little while. It had been years since I last saw my grandma, at least since Mom's funeral. I packed up and hauled Brad into a new adventure. I was going to Britton, South Dakota! Where I was born. Where my grandma and Mom's brothers lived.

I remembered buying a ticket and boarding the bus. I looked out the window wondering what I was thinking, hauling a baby across the country with little money and not telling anyone I was coming.

I could see the scenery passing by as swiftly as my life had passed. It was pitch dark but from what I could see we were somewhere in the desert, moving on, moving forward, to a future of bleakness and uncertainty. I couldn't see my watch in the dark but from the moonlight I guessed it was close to midnight. There was soft snoring from the other passengers and an occasional sneeze. It was the middle of a long night not knowing what tomorrow would bring.

I felt a little disoriented. At that moment on the bus, I couldn't remember where I was or where I was going. I recalled another bus ride less than a year earlier when I returned home from Portland with Brad. The tears were falling down my cheeks and I was scared. What could I have been thinking to pack up my baby and buy that bus ticket, using most of the money I had left? Brad was sleeping soundly next to me, unaware that his mother had taken him on yet another journey, one that would turn into another nightmare!

My mind was fighting to recall the events that led to this trip, but I couldn't remember them. The past year had been hard on the two of us. Trying to make it on our own, with each check welfare graciously doled out to keep us from starving and living in shabby, mouse infested apartments.

At eighteen I should have been partying with my friends and enjoying the last of my teenage years. I loved Brad dearly, but I was too young for the responsibilities of motherhood. The stress of the last few months had been piling up until I was ready to explode. I had to get away. Maybe … Just maybe out of Tacoma I could start a new life with Brad, away from all the memories of the past.

It had been years since I last seen Grandma, but she was the only one I felt close to since Mom's death.

Yes, I had to be on my way to her house, to her warm loving arms. Maybe I could get work there and stay. I'd be near all the relatives I ever wanted and have a family at last! Just maybe ….

"But where am I now and how long will it be until I reach the end of the road."

I was hungry but was low on money, so I decided to skip dinner. I brought enough baby food to feed Brad. I was not too worried about him. I figured I could wait a little longer to eat.

I needed someone to talk to, but all was quiet around me, and I was surrounded by strangers. Looking out the window into the darkness, I saw that we were coming up to a truck stop. The bus was slowing down and pulling into a gas pump lane. After we came to a full stop, the driver announced that we would have a fifteen-minute break. I hated to disturb Brad's sleep, but I had no choice. I needed to stretch and use the bathroom. Cuddling Brad in my arms, I grabbed the diaper bag and made my way down the steps and into the small Café. I immediately headed for the rest room. After changing Brad and washing my hands, I left to get a cup of coffee and to ask the waitress to heat Brad's bottle. Returning to the bus with little time to spare, I settled back into my seat and hoped for sleep to come. The coffee I was sipping as we moved along helped me to relax. After feeding Brad and getting him back to sleep, I was able to at last drift off to sleep.

The sun shining through the bus window woke me up the next morning. Brad was lying in his car seat staring straight ahead, soothed by the motion of the bus. Other passengers stirred and I heard voices in conversation all around me. I was startled by a hand tapping my shoulder and I turned around sharply. An elderly lady asked in a concerned voice,

"Are you OK dear? You look like you need a friend right now."

I smiled weakly but was surprised by her concern and found it difficult to answer. The tears started coming again. I was not used to showing such emotion with strangers but that act of kindness was all it took for me to lose control.

To this day I cannot remember that lady's name, but I can still see her as she moved to the seat beside Brad, trying to comfort me.

"I'm on my way to see my grandma." I told her. "This is my first long trip alone with the baby. I came with very little money, and the baby is tiring me out."

I don't know what made me tell my problems to this stranger. I was just grateful to have someone to talk to that was older than one year.

I found out that we still had another two days on the road. From then on, she took care of Brad's needs, letting me rest. When we stopped for breakfast, the lady took Brad while I freshened up in the bathroom. I was always told not to trust your children with strangers, but I sensed this lady was there to help. When I returned, I saw Brad was laughing and being entertained by every passenger on the bus! He was already fed and changed. He was in good hands and I felt more relaxed than I have been since my trip began. Wanting to save my money, I planned to order only toast, but when I sat at the table with some of the other passengers, I found a big plate of eggs, bacon and steaming coffee waiting for me. Puzzled, I looked at the lady and started to refuse but she insisted that she wanted to help and told me that all the passengers chipped in to buy me breakfast. Not only had they bought my breakfast, but a collection had been taken up while I was gone, to help me continue my trip. I couldn't believe it when she handed me an envelope of money and said, "God be with you."

I cried and thanked her for the generosity she showed me at the darkest moment of my life. I wish to thank all the passengers on that trip to South Dakota so long ago.

The next two days went by swiftly. Everyone made me feel wanted and helped me out with Brad. But the ride soon ended, and everyone parted ways at the bus station, going their own way. Alone again in a strange depot, I clutched Brad close to me and made my way to a phone booth to call Grandma. I hoped someone could pick me up. My uncle Bubber (Robert from birth but was nicknamed Bubber by his whole family) promised to come. While I waited, I had time to think again and wondered just why I was here in a strange town with no friends, no job, and no return ticket.

Suddenly, I heard my name and turned around to find Uncle Bubber coming towards me. Before I knew it, we were embracing. It had been a long time since I'd seen my mom's brother, but I would have known him anywhere. He helped me with my luggage, and we made our way to the car parked outside. There wasn't much room for conversation until we were settled in the seat for the short ride to Grandmas. We started idle chit-chat about how I've grown, how cute Brad was, and how the city had stayed the same ... We talked, but not about the question on both of our minds.

"Why did I come?"

Britton, South Dakota was a farming town, where I was born but never resided, only visited. A place where everyone knew their neighbors, and no one had a secret for long. It was great seeing Grandma. As I hugged her hello, I almost felt my mother's arms around me, comforting me.

It was the middle of summer, hot and humid. I wasn't dressed for this heat and I felt hot and sticky. I couldn't wait until I got unpacked and changed into my shorts. For the first time in weeks, I relaxed and forgot the past, knowing that with Grandma's tender care, I would survive. Brad seemed to love the attention his great-grandma and Uncle Bubber gave him as much as I did.

For two days I did nothing but sleep and eat the great meals Grandma cooked. My favorite times during that visit was sitting at the table with Grandma at night and listen to her reminisce about Mom's childhood. After two weeks, I knew that it was only a visit and I had to move on.

Grandma was in her seventies and the antics of a one year old were trying on her. If it wasn't for all her homegrown vegetables and fresh chickens, she could not have fed us as well as she did. After the first couple days of rest, I walked into town daily to find work, but no one was hiring.

It was a small town consisting of one main street and a handful of stores. The jobs went to the local people. With no experience and no permanent address, no one would hire me. I knew that I had to leave Grandma's house, but how? I had spent all my money coming here and the small donation the passengers on the bus gave me was almost gone. If I wanted to go back to Tacoma I couldn't, not without enough money for a bus ticket.

Out of desperation, I did something that I have always regretted. I stole enough money from Grandma's pocketbook to buy a ticket. As kind as she was, I was willing to do anything to help my son and myself, so I wrote a note saying I had to go home. I vowed as I walked to the bus station that someday I would pay her back.

Uncle Bubber drove me to the bus depot, hugged me goodbye and squeezed my hand, wishing me well. It was only after he left that I noticed the money he had put in my hand,

If I was careful with the money I had, hopefully it would be enough to take us back to Tacoma. The bus arrived and I looked back, only for a minute, picked up Brad and climbed in, settling into our seats.

Fort Hunter Liggett where Dad was stationed near Jolon, California

Ronnie and I during the happiest time of my life.

The general store in front of the trailer park where I lived with Mom, Dad and Jackie in Jolon.

My sister, Jackie's graduation picture.

Mom and Dad

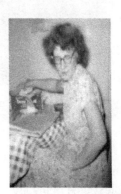

Franklin Pierce High School in Parkland, Washington. I attended school here from 1958-1962. The school included grades 7-12 at the time. I left for Rosemont Home for girls in my senior year. These were the most pleasant of my school years.

This is Bernice and me. Aside from Rose being my first friend, she was the second and last person to be nice to me after I moved to Washington and started attending Franklin Pierce. She remains a very close friend to this day.

Dad with his new wife, Gail. I always felt that I came in second next to Gail. I never got along with her.

American Lake at Fort Lewis, Washington, I would go to this part of the lake during the summers to hang out with the soldiers. This is where I met Jose.

This picture is fuzzy but the only one I had of Lloyd, Brad's father.

My cousin Pat. She was my savior. She helped me escape Rosemont Home for Girls while I was pregnant with Brad, allowing me to keep him. She later gave me a place to stay when I had nowhere else to go.

Kenneth James Moore "Jim" This picture was taken before I met him, just after he joined the Army.

Me with my beloved husband, Jim and my boys, Brad and Allan. This was taken on the day we were married the first time on March 5, 1966. It was our only wedding picture we had taken.

Jim during his time at Walter Reed Hospital. This was taken during the time he was being treated for testicular cancer.

Jim sent this to me right after he was sent to Vietnam. He always tried to make sure I knew he was ok.

Jim and his "Angel".

This is how I remember my Jim. Sleeping in his favorite recliner.

The only family picture taken after Angel joined the family before Jim died.

Echo Glen is a Washington State juvenile detention facility and school operated by the Issaquah school district. The facility has approximately 135 youth in residence, ranging in age from 10 to 20 years old coming from every part of the state. Brad spent a year here. He was fifteen.

Angel in front of the trailer where she lived with Allan. Bill made me find someplace else for them to go as we waited for our house to be built. One of my biggest regrets was letting a man send my kids away.

I took Angel to visit Mom's grave.

This is the house being built. With Bill. What was supposed to be my dream home turned into a nightmare. I lost almost everything I had because of it and had to start over. That is Angela posing in front.

My friend, Gloria. My dad unsuccessfully pursued her.

Me with Vic. Gloria and I followed Elvis impersonator, Vic to all his shows.

This is Twin Rivers prison where Brad was sentenced to 20 year in prison for arson. He got released after 4 years for good behavior and has stayed out of trouble since.

The day Brad graduated while in prison. Given the circumstances, it was one of my proudest moments when I knew Brad was going to be ok.

Allan with his Dad, Syd. Allan finally got to meet his dad in 1993 when he was 28 years old.

My childhood home. Of course, the garlic had been removed years ago. The house was sold in 1992 to the neighbor shortly after Dad passed away. The above picture is my mother with her brother about a month before I lost her. The picture below is me just before the house sold nearly 33 years later.

Chapter 14

Salem, Oregon

1963

The bus trip home was supposed to be smooth sailing. I was going home, back to Tacoma and this time, I planned to stay and work things out. I was through running away from my problems and realized no one else could help me. I was tired of asking for help and being turned down. I would get a job and take care of my son on my own, showing Dad and Gail that I didn't need their help.

Brad sensed another venture ahead and was more hyper than ever, not wanting to sit for a minute. Keeping a close eye on him, I let Brad run as much as he could at the bus station, hoping he would tire himself out and sleep on the bus. As the bus pulled into the parking space, I breathed a sigh of relief, knowing I would be home in a few days.

According to the itinerary I was given with my bus ticket, I was to transfer buses in Salem, and we should get there in two days. Unlike the straight route I took going to South Dakota, I chose to go the cheapest way back home. It meant a day more of traveling and a few more stops, but I was not in any hurry. The time on the bus gave me time to think and plan on what I was going to do when I returned to Tacoma.

Brad slept most of the first day on the bus. He seemed more tired than normal and I could tell he wasn't up to his old self.

"What was I doing to him?"

Dragging him around the country was not good for him and I vowed to my sleeping child that this was the last time. Soon he'd have a home of his own and the best life that I could give him.

The bus was half empty, and unlike the friendly passengers on the last trip, the people on this bus seemed to want to be left alone. I stared out the window at the passing scenery and thought I saw my mother through the window staring back at me with a smile, urging me on. Mom was with me now, if only in a vision and at last I could relax and finally sleep. From now on everything would be okay.

We pulled into a bus stop for a thirty-minute dinner break. Brad was awake by then but awfully quiet. Reaching to pick him up to take him to eat, I noticed he had a fever. I hoped it wasn't serious. What would I do if Brad became sick so far away from home?

I fixed a bottle for him and reached in my purse for some children's aspirin. He didn't seem to want his bottle nor any food, so I ordered a sandwich and a cup of coffee to go. I wasn't hungry at the time and could eat on the bus while Brad slept.

By the next day, Brad seemed to be better and I breathed a sigh of relief that it didn't turn into something worse. I looked at the time. We would soon be arriving in Salem Oregon to change buses. We were halfway home! Another two days and I would see Bernice again! I didn't anticipate seeing Dad or Gail and as far as I knew they could care less if I came back or not.

"Arriving in Salem Oregon in ten minutes. Please start gathering your belongings." The driver announced.

I was startled by his loud voice over the speaker saying that we were almost to Salem. Pulling my bag down from overhead, I grabbed Brad's toys and checked around for anything I might have left behind. I slipped Brad's jacket on him and when the bus pulled into the depot and opened its doors, the two of us made our way to the front of the bus.

I spotted the information booth immediately and asked the girl behind the counter to direct me to the bus going to Tacoma.

"How long do I have?" I asked her.

"The bus is already there and due to pull out in fifteen minutes." The girl informed me.

Quickly making my way to the new bus I fumbled for my purse to retrieve the rest of my ticket home. I felt my side, my front, Brad's lap.

"My purse! Where is my purse? Did I leave it on the bus?"

I had fifteen minutes to find my purse and be on the bus. The ticket, I knew was in my purse and I couldn't get on the bus without it. I backtracked as fast as I could, running and carrying Brad but I was too late, arriving just in time to see the bus pull away from the curb.

"Would someone stop the bus?" I screamed to whoever could hear me.

I ran to find the girl who gave me directions earlier, but no one was there. I glanced at the busses and saw the bus that was to take me home leaving without me. I was stranded with no money, in a strange town. What was I going to do?

I had to think. There had to be a solution. A way out! Someone, somewhere at this bus station that could help me. I was crying and hugging Brad, rocking back and forth on a bench, not caring who saw me and ignoring the stares of the passersby. An hour past, then two. It was getting dark and Brad was restless, but I stayed on that bench as though someone would find me and rescue me.

"Can I help you dear?"

I looked up to see a young woman sitting beside me with concern on her face.

"Is there something I can do?" She asked.

I started to shake my head no, but I needed help. This was a stranger and I have heard of what could happen but was I in a position to turn her away? It was getting dark and I needed help, if not for myself, I needed it for Brad.

"My name is Judy. I just saw my mom off on the bus after a nice visit. I couldn't help but notice that you seem to be upset. Please let me help."

Judy looked to be in her late twenties with blond short hair and slightly overweight. She had a round face and large blue eyes. After hesitating I gasped for air, wiping my eyes. It worked out well for me on the last trip when I trusted that kind lady. I found myself trusting yet another stranger. Before I knew it, I was once again telling a stranger about my plight.

Sobbing I said "I lost my purse with my bus ticket. I need to get home."

After I quieted down, Judy took my hand in hers and assured me that everything would be okay.

"You have a friend now honey, and if you let me, I would like to help you." She said

What choice did I have? At the time, I didn't think there was a way out other than accepting Judy's help. I could call Dad to wire money, but would he? Would he once again refuse to help me? Judy seemed nice enough, someone I could trust. I willingly took her hand as she led me, still holding onto Brad, out of the bus depot, into the darkness of the night.

"You look like you need to eat something, and a good night sleep will do you wonders. I have an extra bedroom and don't live too far from here. Tomorrow we will see what we can do to get you home." She said

I climbed into her car and settled Brad onto my lap. I was tired and maybe after some rest I could come up with a solution to my problem. Maybe my purse would be turned in at the bus depot and I could continue my journey home.

Judy pulled into the driveway of her home. In the dark, I couldn't tell much about the house. It looked like a lonely house, tucked away on a lonely street with no other houses in sight.

"My husband will be home soon from work. I will show you the guest room and let you freshen up while I make dinner for the three of us."

I was scared, shaking and barely uttered a sound.

"What did you get yourself into this time Barbara?" I scolded myself.

Judy pulled into the garage using an automatic garage door opener that was fastened to her visor. The door quickly slammed shut after the car was completely tucked inside.

The guest room was at the top of the stairs. I followed Judy, slowly making my way in that direction, trying not to disturb Brad who was asleep in my arms. I gently placed Brad on the bed and glanced around the small bedroom. There was a full bathroom, a small closet, a full-size bed and a dresser, all of which took up what little space there was. There was something that seemed to be missing, though for a moment I couldn't put my finger on it. As I slowly turned around and looked at the walls, I noticed that there weren't any pictures hanging anywhere, but that wasn't what I found wrong with the room. I stared at the walls, knowing something was amiss, and then it hit me. Bedrooms were supposed to have windows, but there wasn't one single window in that room!

I washed my face and hands, combed my hair, and checked on Brad. He seemed awfully tired and maybe he'd sleep for the rest of the night. I tucked some pillows on both side of him so he wouldn't fall off the bed and tiptoed out of the room, leaving the door open so I could hear him if he should wake up.

I glanced around the front room as followed the sounds of the kitchen heading in that direction. There was a fireplace, small sofa, a rocking chair, a television set, and a large bookcase filled with hundreds of books. As I entered the kitchen I was amazed at the size. It seemed to be as big as the rest of the house combined. Judy had her back to me as she went about her work at the stove. There was a large table in the center of the room, and it was then that I noticed the man sitting with a can of beer in his hand. Judy was overweight, but in comparison to the man, whom I assumed was her husband, she was tiny. He had to weigh at least two hundred and fifty pounds, and even sitting I could tell, he was a rather tall man. He appeared to be at least twenty years older than Judy. His rather scarce hair was grey, and his hands were large. He wore dirty overalls which led me to believe he may work in a garage of some sort, maybe as a mechanic from the grease specks on his face. For some reason, I was frightened of this man and wished more than ever that I had refused Judy's offer to help. Judy at last realized I was standing there and came over to introduce me to her husband.

"Barbara, I'd like you to meet Dan. Dinner is ready so please have a seat."

Dan didn't even glance up to acknowledge the introductions. He kept on reading his evening paper. Dinner was eaten in silence. I wasn't hungry but forced a few bites down. Judy started clearing off the table and I stood up to help her, but Dan stopped me.

"Your company and that's her job! Go into the front room and sit."

Dan sounded like he meant it and though I felt like I should help Judy with the dishes, I knew I had better do as he said. I quickly rushed upstairs to check on Brad, who was still sleeping. Then I joined Dan in the front room.

"Judy told me what happened to you at the bus station. She is always bringing home strays of some sort!"

I was ready to object. I wasn't a stray and I didn't need their help! But I kept quiet.

"You are welcome to stay, but I don't give charity to anyone. You can stay if you wish, but you will work for you and your baby's keep. You will not slouch around on a free ride around here!"

"What was he talking about? I am only here for one night."

I'm planning to be on the bus to Tacoma in the morning, Dan is sounding like I am staying for a longer time.

"Sir, I appreciate your offer, but I plan on returning home tomorrow."

"To what?" Dan asked. "From what Judy told me, you don't have a job waiting for you and no home to go to. Is that what you want for your baby? I'm offering you a job with us as a housekeeper. In return, you will have free room and board and a small allowance. If your careful about your spending, in a few weeks or months you could have enough saved up to start over."

"I'd have to think about it for a while. It's a big move for me and I do have my son to think about. Can I let you know in the morning?"

The offer sounded like what I needed. I was desperate, but I didn't know these people. Dan scared me and I didn't know if I could be around him every day. I hated housework and from looking around at their house, I could tell they would expect things to be in perfect shape. But Dan was right. What did I have waiting for me back in Tacoma? A dad who could care less, no job or money, a life of welfare and struggling to get by. Maybe a start in completely new surroundings was what I needed.

I had a lot to think about and knew I wouldn't get much sleep tonight. I sat in a chair beside the bed and watched Brad sleep, listening to the clock ticking as time passed by.

"What am I going to do?"

I didn't understand why complete strangers would offer to take someone in who they knew nothing about. I was torn in two directions, wanting to go home to see Bernice and yet, I knew that staying here would probably be for the best. Brad has been uprooted so many times in his short life. By the end of the night, I decided I must remain here for a while longer. Since my room and board would be taken care of, I would save whatever allowance given to me until I had enough to complete my journey home.

Morning at last came. I was still sitting in the same position as last night. I was sore and my head ached. Maybe a bath was what I needed. Just as I was finishing up in the shower, I heard Brad stir and knew the first day of my new life started!

Quickly, I changed Brad and the two of us went downstairs to the smell of coffee brewing and bacon frying. Judy was standing at the stove and Dan was sipping coffee at the table. He was dressed for work and had the same frown on his face as he did last night.

"Doesn't he ever smile?" I thought to myself.

I helped myself to a cup of coffee and fixed Brad a bottle. Then I seated myself at the table next to Dan.

"Well, have you thought about my offer?" Dan asked.

"I thought of nothing else last night, and I know that accepting the job is the best thing for me, with the understanding I can leave at any time."

"I am glad you have decided to stay with us, and you most certainly can leave any time you wish. I would like some advance notice, however, so I can get someone else. We both work and it's been hard on her to cook, clean and go to work. You will be alone here every day and have complete charge of running things around here. I expect the house to remain clean, the laundry kept up, and a decent meal when the two of us come home at night. Judy will continue fixing breakfast to give you time to dress and feed the baby. Judy has a couple of days off from work and will show you what is expected."

I nodded to him but didn't say a word. We ate breakfast in silence and then Dan was off to work. At least

I would have the days free from facing him. Getting the house to myself everyday didn't seem all that bad either.

After Dan left, Judy took Brad from me and sat at the table with him in her lap.

"He's a precious boy. You should be very proud to be his mom."

I saw the far away yearning in her eyes and wondered to myself why she didn't have any children. Judy interrupted my thoughts.

"I have a crib and highchair stored in the attic. I even think there may be some clothes that will fit him. After the dishes are done, we'll go see what we can find."

I wondered if there was a baby who lived here at some time. Otherwise, why would there be baby items in storage. I helped Judy with the dishes and then we were off to the attic. Just as she said, there were a lot of things that would do nicely. Brad had a ball playing in the corner with some toys he found. I couldn't believe anyone's attic would be so spotless, but it was as clean as the rest of the house. We found the baby furniture and a box of toys. The box of clothes I would go thru later and wash the ones I could use.

"Where was the baby who once made use of these things" I thought to myself.

By the time we hauled everything downstairs and set up the crib, it was lunch time and Brad's crying told me it was his nap time as well. Over sandwiches and coffee, Judy and I finally had a chance to talk and get to know each other a little better.

"Dan is not as tough as he seems. I hope he didn't intimidate you. If you keep the house nice and have his meals ready, he should leave you alone. I will do the shopping and there should be plenty of food here at all times, so do help yourself."

I enjoyed the two days Judy was home. It was like having a sister to talk to, but soon she was heading for work and at last, I was alone. The work was not that hard, and I managed to find time in the day to spend with Brad. I stayed out of Dan's way as much as I could. The only time I saw him was at dinner. At night he would retire to the front room and I would go to my room to read or to play with Brad. A week flew by faster than I expected with nothing significant happening. I was starting to relax and enjoy the time I had with my son without worrying where our next meal would come from.

The second week started out just like the first week did, with one exception. Dan talked to me more and was sounding a little friendlier. Treating me like a person and not like I was invisible as he did the week before. I also noticed that Judy would leave the house after dinner at night, leaving her husband and me alone for long periods of time. She either had to go to the store or visit a friend. At the time, I didn't think anything unusual about it.

During the time that Judy was gone in the evening, I noticed that Dan was friendlier than ever. Maybe it was my imagination, but I sensed that something was very different in the way he looked and spoke to me. He would insist that I join him in the front room after dinner. Because of the lack of seating, I was forced to sit next to him on the sofa. His leg would rub against mine and his hands slowly moving my way.

"Do you know why Judy has been leaving us alone so much?" Dan asked one night. "It's so we can get better acquainted."

I stared at him, wondering just where he was headed with this conversation.

"I'm a lonely man. I have Judy and love her very much, but she hasn't been able to give me what I need the most. Because Judy loves me, she wants to do anything she can to please me, even if it means sharing me with someone else. That's where you come in."

I sat there with my mouth open, but unable to speak. Was he saying what I think he was?

"I crave sex all the time and Judy can't seem to give me enough of it. Rather than cheating on her and looking elsewhere, we have a mutual agreement that I keep my affairs in the open as well as in the house. You're young and single and we can please each other. I will continue to give you and your son a home here for a long as you want. In return, I expect you to fulfill my needs."

I knew at that moment what Dan had in mind. How was I going to get out of this one?

"If you're suggesting what I think you are, Dan, I'm leaving right now. No way would I agree to that. I can't believe Judy would go along with it."

"You really have no choice. You must think about your baby. In a flash, I could have him taken away from you. You are unable to provide a home for him and the way he is moved around the country will convince any judge that your unfit to care for him. I am well respected in this town and the courts will listen to me."

I tried not to cry but the tears came.

"You wouldn't take a baby away from its mother, would you?"

"Try and fight me on this and you will see. Do you want to take the risk?"

I started to rise from the couch. I wanted to run, but where would I go. Dan got up and started walking toward me, backing me against the wall.

"Judy won't be home for a while. I want to see just what I am getting in the bargain."

Dan put his arms around my neck and held me against the wall. No one would hear me if I screamed and I didn't want to wake Brad up. I didn't want him to witness what Dan was planning to do with his mother. Dan was a big man as well as strong and I was no match for him. With one hand pinning me down, the other hand ripped my blouse off. Suddenly he picked me up and carried me towards his and Judy's bedroom. I kicked and shoved, but because my son sleeping so close by, I remained silent.

"This is new for you so this time I will put up with your fighting, but next time, you better be more willing… if you want to keep your son."

Dan ripped what remaining clothes I had on and started touching me with his rough dirty hands. With one hand still holding me down he quickly removed his clothes. His mouth was on mine and the smell of stale smoke and alcohol was making me sick. His mouth was exploring my whole body and I knew it would do no good to fight, so I closed my eyes and pretended I was safe at home in Tacoma. Dan climbed up over my head and forced his penis into my mouth causing me to gag. I had never had a man do that before. It was huge, hard and sticky and it felt like he was pushing it to the furthest part of my throat. I couldn't breathe. Eventually he pulled it from me and lowered himself in position to enter my body. He groaned and cussed as he went up and down. He acted like an animal in heat, like he had not had sex in a long time. When he was done, he pulled himself from me and lit a cigarette.

"It wasn't bad for the first time, but you will improve with time. There are so many ways I like to do it and I want to be your teacher. Don't worry about getting pregnant, I can't have children. I expect you to be ready when I say, day or night. If I feel the need and Judy's not around, you will be. Understand?"

I was in shock and very sore. I climbed out of his bed, picked up my clothes, and without a word went back to my room. As I left, I heard him yell behind me, "By the way, don't plan on running. There's nowhere to go. And remember just how much you love your son and want to keep him!"

I checked on Brad, covered him up then headed for the shower. Once again, I was reminded of the rape so long ago. Will this ever end for me? I climbed into bed and cuddled my pillow like a child. What was I going to do? How could Judy go along with this? Maybe Dan just said she knew. If I told her what happened, maybe she would help me.

I stayed in bed later than usual hoping Dan would've gone to work. When I finally had to force myself downstairs because Brad was awake and demanding his breakfast, I found Judy doing the breakfast dishes and Dan gone. I fixed a bottle for Brad and poured some coffee for me. Judy sat beside me. I noticed her staring at me in a strange way. I could tell that she knew what happened the night before.

"I don't have to go to work today. I don't feel too well and called in sick. I understand that Dan talked to you last night?"

I couldn't believe she supported Dan in this crazy scheme.

121

"How could you let your husband treat me that way?"

"Dan and I talked it over for a long time and we both agreed it would be good for our marriage. We were on the verge of breaking up and to save our marriage I agreed to at least try it his way. When I saw you at the bus station, I knew you were the answer to our prayers."

"He raped me and that's illegal. There are probably a lot of girls out there who would do it willingly so why force me?"

"Dan enjoys a little fight and we knew since you had the baby here, we could get you to do what we asked. Oh yes, now that Dan has initiated you, I won't have to leave anymore. You see, it turns Dan on when I watch him make it with another woman."

Was this a dream? How can anyone get their thrills that way?

"I have a doctor's appointment, but I shouldn't be long. I will stop on the way home to pick up some baby food for Brad and some groceries for us."

When the door closed behind her, I started checking the drawers for any money stashed. Maybe I could be gone before she came home. I only found a few pennies but decided to leave anyway. There had to be someone out there that could help me. I packed Brad's things and made my way to the front door. It was locked! Judy locked me in. I checked the windows and back door. Everything was locked. There was no way out! The phone. I picked it up and tried to dial but there was no dial tone. I was trapped! A prisoner in this house!

I spent the rest of the day in my bedroom. Judy came home and soon after, I heard Dan. I cringed at the sound of his voice, but they left me alone that night. I could hear the two of them in their room making love and I breathed a sigh of relief. Judy was satisfying him tonight.

For two days nothing happened. Dan left me alone, but they continued to lock me in when they went to work. If it wasn't for Brad, I would have found a way out, but for him I would do what it took to get us both out of this mess.

On the third night I was sitting on my bed trying to read when the door opened, and Dan walked in. By the look on his face I knew that it was the time I was dreading. It would do no good to fight. For a short while, I would do what he asked but while I was alone in the daytime, I would find a way out. Dan motioned for me to come and I knew if I did not go willingly, he would again force me. I felt defeated. I stood to follow him for whatever lies ahead.

"You know what to do, so get undressed, unless you want me to take your clothes off again. And you had better be more cooperative this time!"

Silently I removed my clothes as Dan removed his and then he reached for me and started kissing me, pushing me onto the bed.

"No, please don't." I started to cry out, but he silenced me with his lips.

"Tonight, we will do something different. Something I have wanted to try for a long time. I have always wondered what it would be like to have more than one girl at a time. Well, I have two girls in the house now and I might as well see what you both can do. Judy get in here!"

In walked Judy from the bathroom, naked! In a flash, she was on the bed with us touching Dan all over while he was fondling me. I had heard about group sex before but didn't really believe there were people like that around, but now I was experiencing it first-hand! I tried to do what he wanted but I didn't know exactly what that was, so he had to guide me, pushing my hands where he wanted them. Again, Dan climbed over my head and found my mouth while Judy's hands fondle us both. I cringed and closed my eyes wanting this to be over, but I had a feeling it had just begun.

How can one man have so much energy? He lowered himself over Judy while kissing me. he would pump on her for a while then switched to me until he eventually came, sharing his semen with us both.

"Judy you go sleep in Barbara's room tonight. I want her here with me for a while longer."

Oh God, wasn't he going to let me go? I don't want to spend the whole night with this monster, but Judy obeyed, and we were alone. Soon Dan was snoring beside me as I laid there crying, wondering when this nightmare would ever end.

Twice that night Dan woke up and grabbed for me. Each time it was quick, long enough to satisfy him. That night seemed to never end but eventually the sunlight came thru the window and the alarm clock was ringing telling me it was time for Dan to go to work. Brad should be waking up soon and I didn't want him to see me this way, so I got out of bed and went to the bathroom to shower, scrubbing every inch of my body that had been touched by the two of them.

Every third day Dan would summon me. Sometimes it would be the two of us, but more often Judy would join in. In the daytime, I searched frantically for a way out. I pried and scraped at the windows using whatever I could find as a tool. I picked at the locks and tried breaking a window but no luck. They intended on keeping me here until they tired of me, but would they let me go even then? There was no way out.

Three months past. The routine was the same week after week. Dan never seemed to tire of me, and Judy never would defy her husband. Then it hit me, a plan that might work!

I stopped complaining when I had to go to Dan's room, and I pretended to enjoy what he was doing to me. I helped Judy more around the house, finally convincing them that I had at last accepted my life with them.

After a month of getting closer to the two of them, I decided it was time to test my plan.

"Judy you work hard and shouldn't have to do all the grocery shopping. I am beginning to like my life here. There's no need to lock me in any longer. If you let me, I'd be happy to take over some of the outdoor chores. Besides Brad needs some fresh air. He hasn't been outside in months."

"I don't know," Judy responded. "Dan wouldn't like that."

"Do you have to get Dan's permission for everything you do? You look worn out and I feel I'm not earning my keep around here. If you want, Dan wouldn't even have to know. I can do the shopping early enough and be back before he gets home from work."

Judy looked like she was ready to give in. I could tell she needed the help. She hated shopping and I think the idea of doing something behind her husband's back appealed to her.

"Okay, we will give it a try. I think I could trust you not to run after all this time. You are right, Brad does need to get outside. Maybe tomorrow we will give it a try."

I hoped it would work. If I get caught, she won't trust me again and my only chance for escape will be gone. If Judy doesn't change her mind by tomorrow or tell Dan. I secretly packed what few belongings Brad and I had, taking nothing that was given to us by Dan or Judy, hiding what I packed under the bed.

"Please let this work." I prayed.

Morning was the same as any other morning. Dan was reading the paper while Judy prepared his breakfast.

"I have to buy groceries today Dan. Anything you especially want?" She asked.

Dan looked up from his paper, thought a moment and replied, "Get plenty of beer. I'm also out of cigarettes." He tossed her a wad of bills to pay for the things he wanted.

After Dan left for work, Judy cleaned the kitchen in silence then went to the bathroom to get ready for work. The suspense was killing me. Will she trust me enough to do the shopping?

When Judy returned, she sat at the table beside me.

"I have a few moments before I leave. You must promise me that you will do the shopping and come right back home. If anything happens and Dan finds out, we will both pay!"

I assured her she could trust me and was given a list of groceries to buy. "This is rather a long list, too long for you to carry home with the baby. I'll add enough for you to get a cab to bring you home. Here is a spare key for the house. I'll check on you in three hours to make sure you're back. You better be!"

Three hours to run as fast as I can. It doesn't give me much time. At least I was packed. I waited about thirty minutes after Judy left to make sure she wasn't watching me or would return home. I hurriedly changed Brad and threw some formula and food from the kitchen in my bag. For the first time in three months, I found myself outside smelling the fresh air. I was thankful it was a warm day. Judy gave me one hundred dollars for groceries. I hoped that was enough for a bus ticket to somewhere safe.

I walked for about a mile and spotted a city bus stop. The bus was just pulling up. I explained to the driver that I was new in town and wanted to go to the greyhound bus station. Within thirty minutes he was pulling in front of the station to let me off. Once inside the depot I made my way to the ticket agent, crossing my fingers, hoping that I had enough money and that the wait for the bus would not be long. A ticket to Tacoma would be fifty dollars and would leave in thirty minutes. Maybe I would be on the bus and out of town before Judy discovered I was gone!

It never once entered my mind to go to the police. The fear of Dan's threat was still with me and I was afraid I'd lose my son. I fought to keep my baby when I was at Rosemont, I was not going to lose him now!

I was on the bus heading home at last! I vowed no matter what the future held I would remain in Tacoma. I was done with running away.

I would not trust another stranger! I was going home. I didn't know what was ahead of me, but the past was behind me. Brad and I would be safe. I'd see to it. Somehow, we'd be alright.

Chapter 15

A man named Syd

1964

I had only been back from Salem for three months. After spending a few weeks with Bernice, I found an apartment not far from her. With my first welfare check, Brad and I at last moved into our own place. Brad finally had a bedroom of his own and a small yard to play in. I was close enough to my best friend to visit as often as I wanted. By this time Bernice had a daughter of her own and we were able to babysit for each other, giving us each time to get away for a while. For the first time in years, things seemed to be looking up for me.

Friday nights I would leave Brad with Bernice, or a sitter if she wasn't available and go out. I wanted to escape motherhood and be a teenager, even if it was for one night be week.

I decided to try a dancing club in town that was recommended by a neighbor in my apartment building. Jan went there often and after finding out how much I loved to dance, offered to take me with her. It was a large club with a live band, playing all the songs I loved. I didn't think anyone would ever ask me to dance, but much to my delight, I danced more that night then I have ever danced in my life. Every Friday night, after that first night, I started venturing out to the club alone.

It was the fourth Friday night that I saw him. He was sitting alone at the bar, holding a beer, and listening to the music. He seemed to be alone and from my observation, he seemed out of place.

"Another lonely person," I thought to myself,

The music was kind of depressing that night, the band sang of lost loves, dying, or being alone. After a couple of hours of depressing music and not much to dance to, I decided as soon as I finished my drink I would leave. Someone requested that the band play the song Last dance. I loved that song and found myself singing along.

"May I have this dance?"

Startled I turned around sharply and there he was. The stranger at the bar, standing there in front of me. He had beautiful blond curly hair, round face, and was about five feet, eight inches tall. He stood like a soldier would, at attention, with his hand held out to me.

I wasn't in the mood to dance and was ready to turn him down, but something told me I would be sorry if I did, so I took his hand and let him lead me to the dance floor.

"You look as lost as I feel. I don't even know why I'm here. At least I didn't until now." He said.

I looked slowly into the stranger's eyes and saw the pain there. I also saw something else, something I haven't seen in a long time. A man's desire. I was speechless and had to search for something to say.

"I don't really know why I'm here either. I was getting ready to leave when you came over."

"It's early yet and since we are both bored, can I take you next door for a cup of coffee?" He said.

"I don't usually go off with strange men. I don't even know your name." I told him.

"My name is Sydney and I've never asked a strange girl out for coffee in my life. And just who am I asking out anyway?" Syd asked with a smile.

"My name is Barbara. I'm glad to meet you Syd. And now that we're no longer strangers, I would love to get out of this place."

I knew going outside with Syd could put me in another dangerous situation. It was dark and I knew nothing about him, but something told me he was different. After the dance ended, I picked my purse up and walked with him to the happiest nine months I have ever known before.

For two hours that first night we talked and shared things about each other, getting to know each other better. Syd was in the army, stationed at Fort Lewis. He was from a small town in Oregon. He talked a lot about his mom and dad. I could see he was homesick in his eyes as he talked about them. He told me that he hardly ever left the barracks, but he was tired of listening to his roommates, so decided to go out for a while.

I told him about Brad, hoping that having a child wouldn't chase him the other way. By the end of the night, I gave him my phone number, hoping he would call me, but having very little confidence that he would.

Two days past and Syd didn't call. I was beginning to wonder if he decided to avoid me after all, maybe he forgot about me already. On the third day, the call came. I was twenty years old, but at that moment, I felt like a young teenager, getting her first phone call from a boy! Syd asked me out but because of the short notice and no babysitter, I invited him over for dinner.

I fed Brad early and got him ready for bed, but I let him stay up long enough to meet Syd. After introducing my son to him, I let the two guys get acquainted while I finished dinner. Tucking Brad into bed that night, I kissed him and whispered, "This could be the, honey. Maybe we can now be happy, at last."

I returned to the front room and found Syd pouring wine into two glasses. He seemed to enjoy my dinner. I wasn't sure just how enjoyable it was since I was so nervous that I hardly tasted the food that night. I was afraid I might say or do something wrong. Afraid I might blow this one chance of happiness. Syd was very quiet also, so we ate in silence. I silently wondered just how the night would end.

After dinner, we returned to the front room and Syd asked if he could turn the television on. We sat and watched a movie together. I could feel him beside me, wishing he would put his arm around me. I didn't want to rush things. I wanted Syd to make the first move when the time was right. When the movie ended Syd got up from the couch and stretched.

"I really enjoyed dinner Barbara. I especially liked the company, but I have to get up early for work. As much as I hate to, I'm going to have to go. I hope we can do this again real soon."

I escorted him to the door, assuring him that I also had a good time. I was hoping that he would kiss me goodbye but maybe I was expecting too much. Maybe Syd was just a lonely soldier looking for a home cooked meal. As I closed the door behind him, I had the feeling I wouldn't hear from him again. The phone ringing the next day would tell me otherwise. He wanted to see me again! I was hoping he would ask me out dancing or to dinner, but he suggested bringing over some steaks and having a repeat date from the night before.

While watching television that night, Syd put his arms around me and during commercial he reached over and kissed my neck. I slowly turned around until our eyes met and he pulled me close to him for a long kiss. My heart fluttered and my hands shook. I could not ever remember feeling like I did at that moment with any other man. As the kiss came to an end, I knew this was the man I wanted in my life forever. It didn't matter that we had only known each other for a week. I felt it was right and hoped Syd felt the same way. We watched the remainder of the movie snuggling together, only kissing during commercials and I thought it couldn't get any better than it was that night.

Syd came over every night that week, sometimes bringing dinner with him. Other times I would cook, but we never went out. Though I wondered why, I never asked him if we could go anywhere. We never did much more than kiss that first week and I would have been content if we ventured no further. I was nervous and still afraid of sex. I wasn't sure of what I would do when Syd would expect more. The kisses eventually became more, and Syd began exploring my body. I stiffened and wanted him to stop but I was afraid he would pull away from me and never return. Syd was showing me the love I craved and if sex was part of the package I would pretend. In my mind, by pretending, Syd would love me forever and I would never be alone again. Rockets were supposed to explode, lights were supposed to flash, and the earth was supposed to stand still as we slowly explored our bodies, but things were the same for me. I felt no different and as Syd reached a climax, I heaved a sigh of relief. Though he thought my groans were that of satisfaction, only I knew it was relief that it was over. Syd tried to make me happy. He was gentle but every time his hands touched my body I cringed and, in my mind, saw Joe's and Dan's hands on me. I became good at pretending to like the sex. I knew if I didn't, I would be alone again knowing that to be loved, sex would have to be a part of it. I was hoping to fool Syd but, in the end, realizing that I was fooling only myself.

After that night Syd was at my house every moment that he didn't have to work. The routine never changed. Dinner, television, sex and sleeping was our daily schedule in that order. Syd talked about his folks in Oregon often. As soon as he got out of the army, he wanted to head home. A few times he talked about me going with him, but as much as I cared for him, I had my doubts about leaving Tacoma, remembering my vow to Brad when I returned from Salem. I promised him I would never take him away for the unknown again. As the weeks turned into months there was something else that bothered me, keeping me from making a permanent commitment to him.

Syd never once in the months we were together, took me out. He was content staying home watching television. His constant talk about his mother made me feel I was a replacement for his family. He mentioned marriage a few times, besides the fact I was still legally married to Lloyd, I couldn't shake the feeling that Syd thought of me more as a mother figure than his girlfriend.

With Syd in the army, I knew the inevitable would eventually happen and we would be separated. He had already been at Fort Lewis for twelve months and we knew it would someday be time to him to move on. It happened sooner then I wanted, and I was not prepared to say good-bye. He told me he had orders for Okinawa, and we had four more weeks together. I wanted to cry. I wanted our last week's together to be perfect, filled with happiness and not sorrow, so I held the tears back. I chose not to tell him my secret, a secret that he would not be able to do anything about. The army will wait for no one. I didn't want him to leave the country and I didn't want him to leave worried about me, so I remained silent. I didn't tell him I was pregnant with his child.

Our last night together was perfect. Neither of us wanted to talk about his leaving. Bernice watched Brad for

133

the night, and I fixed a beautiful dinner complete with candles. After dinner, we turned the radio on. We listened to music and cuddled on the couch.

Last Dance was playing, and Syd took my hand in his. He pulled me to my feet so we could dance to the music. The song in which was our first dance when we met was now to be our last dance together. We made love that night like we both knew it would be our last time. Though neither said anything, we both had a feeling that he would not return.

After Syd left, life went on as it did before I knew him, except now I was pregnant. I didn't want to be on welfare but had little choice. I reported my pregnancy to DSHS. My check increased with the pregnancy and I started seeing a doctor. The baby was fine and due to be born sometime in January.

For three months after Syd left, I wrote him daily. He still mentioned marriage and wanted me to meet his parents. He also wrote about the two of us living with his mom. Never did he mention getting a place of our own. Even in letters I never told him about the baby. Eventually the letters slowed down to weekly until they quit altogether. I knew then that it was over. I now had two children to care for and I was more determined than ever to make a better life for them.

Chapter 16

I'm a Nanny

1965

.

      This pregnancy was almost stress free, unlike when I was pregnant with Brad, because at least I had a home and some money. Though I hated being on welfare, it was better than being on the street. I wasn't sick with this pregnancy, nor did I gain much weight. Vowing to keep my promise to Brad and my unborn child, I was going to get off from welfare and make my children proud of me, so when I spotted the help wanted sign in the local supermarket, I wrote down the number. It was a live-in nanny position with room and board, some spending money and medical, but would they consider a two-year old and a pregnant nanny. Probably not, but it wouldn't hurt to call.

      The woman on the other end of the phone seemed excited that I called, as if I was her last resort.

      "I've had a lot of calls on the position, but as soon as I mention I have seven kids, they hung up. Please don't say no until you meet with me."

      I heard the desperation in her voice, and I needed the job, but seven kids? With Brad, there would be eight children in my care. "Could I do it?"

      "I might be interested but there's something you should know about me first. You may be the one to hang up." I told her. "First, I have a two-year old son, and second, I am three months pregnant. I would be very interested in the job if you can accept me under those conditions. Of course, I would accept less to compensate for my son's living expenses. I really need the job and I do

135

love children. So, if you would still like to meet me, just name the time."

There was a short hesitation on the other end while she thought about what I said.

"I see no problem with that, but first I want you to meet the children to see if you really want to face them daily. Can you come over this afternoon?"

After writing down the directions and setting the time, we said goodbye. I was already starting to have second thoughts about showing up for the appointment, but as time grew closer, I knew I'd be there. If they still wanted me, I would take the job. Brad would have lots of children to play with, a large house and a yard. I could do it for my son.

I had to take the city bus and walk a few more blocks to get there but I made it on time.

Wanda lived on Fort Lewis, so I knew either she or her husband was in the army. As I got closer, I discovered she lived less than two blocks from the park. Brad would really love that. The weather was getting warmer and I could spend a lot of time at the lake with the children. The house was the last one on the road surrounded by trees. It was a beautiful neighborhood with yards that looked picture perfect. All the houses were duplexes. Each were separated by a carport. I knew I would love it here. As I approached the house I was looking for, I became excited.

"Oh, please let me get this job" I pleaded to myself.

Wanda answered the door and ushered me to the front room.

"I'm glad you were able to find the place. Can I get you anything to drink?" She asked.

As I waited for Wanda to return with a glass of water, I glanced around the room. There was a fireplace, and a sliding glass door looking out onto a beautiful patio. The lake could be seen from the window. I thought it seemed awfully quiet considering there should have been the noise of seven children. I wondered where they were.

Wanda was average looking, and her weight was appropriate for her height. She had black, wavy shoulder length hair, and smooth silky skin. I wondered how anyone could look as good as she did after having seven children.

"The kids are at the park with the neighbors." As if she could read my mind.

"I thought it would be best if we talked first before you meet them. My husband is in the army and at work right now, but he said he would abide by my decision. I have three girls and four boys. The oldest is fourteen. He's the one you should know more about. You see, Dwayne is mentally handicapped and has the maturity of a four-year-old. I work as a secretary at Rainier School for the handicapped and Dwayne accompanies me there daily. He shouldn't be a problem for you."

"I understand." I replied. "I can't wait to meet the children."

"They'll be back shortly. The children are a handful, so I don't expect you to slave over housework. Just pick up after yourself, help me with dinner and dishes, and sort of keep the house in order as much as you can while I'm at work. After you meet the kids, the job is yours if you still want it."

"I think I've already decided but you do remember about my son and pregnancy. I know you said on the phone it didn't make a difference, but have you thought any more about it?" I asked her.

Wanda smiled, "Dear, I'd love to have another child in the house. As you can tell, I love kids and one more would be wonderful. As for your pregnancy, if you can keep up with the kids, it shouldn't be a problem."

When the kids returned home, we were talking like we were old friends. The back-door slamming told me our privacy would soon be invaded. In came seven of the cutest children I have ever seen. As I inspected each one, I knew which one Dwayne was without being introduced. He stood behind his siblings with his finger in his mouth, dripping water from his swimming suit onto the rug. I knew at that moment that I wanted to be a part of these kids' lives.

Wanda stood beside her children and started to introduce me to them separately. Tina at four years of age, was the youngest. I had the feeling that she and Brad would become best friends.

After the short visit with the kids, Wanda asked them to play in the back yard.

"Well?" she asked glancing my way.

"They are adorable, and I'd love to take care of them."

"Great. Let me show you to your room. We will discuss salary and other issues later."

Wanda led me to the back of the house, to a large room at the end.

"This room is large enough for you and Brad to share. There are four bedrooms. The girls share one and the boys share the other. You have your own bathroom. If you want, you can move in tonight. My husband has a truck and can help you get your things."

138

And so, I became a nanny by trade, and a big sister to seven children who needed me. Wanda's husband, Greg, was wonderful. He made me feel like a part of the family from the moment we met. I felt like I had at last the loving family I'd always wanted.

That summer was the best summer I could ever remember. Brad loved the house and yard and as I expected, he idolized Tina. He followed her around wherever she went. Daily, I would get up in the morning, clean my room, fix breakfast for the kids, get them dressed in their swimming suits, pack picnic lunches and head for the park. I would read or swim with the kids, play ball, and just have fun in the sun. We would arrive home in time to start dinner at night. When the fall came, it became cooler so we would stay at home and play games, watch television, or I would read to them. They grew to love and trust me and to really consider me their big sister.

Winter came and the ice and snow followed. Thanksgiving that year reminded me of old times when Mom was still alive. A large table with all the turkey we could eat and eight children with three adults, holding hands praying. Tears came to my eyes as I glanced around the table, feeling like I was truly a part of their family.

Christmas was a big affair that year. Wanda and Greg taught their kids the real meaning of Christmas, so it didn't matter that they received fewer gifts. Being together, singing carols, baking pies together, meant more to those children than any gifts they could have received. As Christmas came, I realized that soon I would have another baby to care for and wondered if I would be able to stay with them after I give birth.

I had never celebrated New Year's Day the way this family did. It was Thanksgiving all over again with a turkey meal. While the girls cooked, the boys watched football together. We would all sit down around the table and start the New Year as a family should, together.

The prayers ended and Greg started to carve the turkey. It was then that the pain started. I was in labor or at least I thought I was. I remembered the same pain when I had Brad. I fought it and held back the screams, though I wanted to grab a hold of the nearest two kids. I was determined not to ruin the best New Years I have ever had, and the meal looked so delicious, I did not want to deny myself the luxury of such a feast, so I held my chair with each pain and continued eating. Babies take hours to be born and I knew there would be plenty of time to finish the meal.

Shoving the last of the pumpkin pie into my mouth, I could not withhold the pain any longer. It was getting harder and I felt water dripping down my legs.

"Wanda, I think I had better get to the hospital unless you want me to have this baby at your dining room table."

Greg rushed out to warm up the car while Wanda grabbed my bag. She had to remain with the kids, so it was Greg who took me to the hospital. It was an easy birth and eight hours later, on New Year's Day, 1965, my son, Allan was born. After three days in the hospital, I was able to take my son home to meet his brother, Brad.

My bedroom was a little more crowded having to share it now with two kids. Brad moved into the bed with me and Allan took over the crib, which Brad was too old for anyway.

Wanda and Greg were wonderful through it all and offered to let me continue with them if I wanted. I tried but Allan made nine children to care for. I was exhausted.

Allan kept me busy so I couldn't spend quality time with the other children. One month after Allan's birth, I reluctantly gave Wanda my resignation. I apologized to them both for leaving them in a bind, but they understood and wished me well. I stayed with them for two more weeks while I found an apartment and got back on welfare. It was a sad day when I left. Brad cried when he had to leave Tina, but it was for the best, and so once again, we were on our own.

Chapter 17

Love at last!

1966

I often wondered through the years if Syd knew he had a son, would it have made a difference. Would we have married and lived happily ever after?

After I moved out from Wanda's and got my own place, I decided to write a letter to Syd's company commander in Okinawa after Allan was born. I wasn't sure if he would still be there. I hoped my letter would find him. In the short letter, I explained that I had a baby and Syd was the father. I made it clear I wanted no support, but that I thought Syd would want to know he had a son. I hung onto that letter for a week before I mailed it.

One month later, I received a letter from Okinawa. My heart skipped a beat, thinking that it would be from Syd. Was he happy about the baby? Would he come find us when he returned?

"Please let it be good news!" I whispered to myself.

It was a one-page letter from the company commander. I was deeply disappointed when I saw I wasn't from Syd. The letter was short and to the point, telling me that he talked to Syd and told him about the baby.

"I'm sorry miss, but the soldier in question denies being the father and said there were many men you were with. He further states that it could be somebody else's baby."

I couldn't believe what I read. That wasn't the Syd I remembered. I now have another son who will never know his father. It was time to move on.

The next few months after leaving Wanda's were difficult. Allan needed more attention than Brad did as a baby. I was up with him half the night, then I had to chase a rambunctious two-year-old around by day. I found a nice two-bedroom house in a low-income housing project. It had a fenced yard and lots of children in the neighborhood for Brad to play with. I had no money to go out and Bernice lived too far away to see too often, so I stayed home and took care of my two boys.

While at the grocery store one day I felt a tap on my back and heard a very familiar voice behind me.

"Barbara, is that really you?"

Startled, I quickly turned around, almost dropping the jar of pickles I was holding. Brad was standing in the grocery cart demanding everything in sight, and Allan was asleep in the basket while I tried rushing through my weekly grocery shopping chore.

I stared at the woman who called my name. She looked so familiar, but I couldn't at first recall where I knew her from. Then the years flew backwards to my childhood. She was older and had gained a lot of weight but after taking a second look, I knew that my first best friend in school had returned. It was Rose. The first one to be friendly towards me when I left Jolon and moved to Tacoma. I reached out my arms to give my old friend a hug. As we cried together, we forgot for a moment about our children who by then were screaming for attention. Rose had two children with her, a boy and a girl, just a little older than my two. They seemed to be competing with Allan and Brad to see who can be the loudest.

143

Rose laughed as she tried to talk above the kid's noise,

"I can see the kids won't let us talk right now. I live just around the corner so why don't you come over for a cup of coffee and we can catch up on our lives?"

The two of us loaded the kids into Rose's car and headed to her place. As we approached her house, I realized that she lived only two blocks from me.

It was a beautiful day, so we put the kids in her back yard to play and sat on her patio with glasses of cold lemonade instead of coffee.

"I can't believe it's really you, Rose. And to think, you live so close to me!" I commented as she sat down with drinks in hand.

"We just moved back to Tacoma a month ago because my husband got stationed at Fort Lewis. I was hoping you'd still be in town."

We exchanged news about ourselves, admiring each other's children. I wanted to tell her all that had happened to me, but I didn't want to spoil the moment. It was a happy occasion and I hoped there would be plenty of time later to talk about myself. I listened to Rose talk happily about her husband, James. I couldn't help feeling a little envious of her. It sounded like she was the one who made a happy life for herself. A life I was still yearning for and though I didn't want to think that way, I was feeling a little resentment because of what she had, and I didn't.

We were enjoying being together so much that the time flew by. I didn't realize it was so late until Brad started fussing for his dinner, so as much as I wanted to stay; I needed to get my boys home. Rose piled the kids in the car and drove me home. As we parted, we promised to keep in touch.

Rose called me the next day and I invited them over for lunch. I was excited to have a friend so close to home and the boys had new friends to play with as well. Eager to entertain, I busily cleaned house and made up some sandwiches for lunch. I found myself singing as I worked. Something I hadn't done in a long time.

The weeks flew by and I saw Rose as often as possible. After a few days, I finally met her husband. James was a tiny man, not weighing more than one hundred and thirty pounds. He was older than Rose by about twelve years, but I could tell how devoted he was to her and the children. From the very first day I met James, he made me feel like a part of his family.

James decide I needed a man and that the boys needed a father, so he took it upon himself to find a mate for me. Every chance he got; he would "accidentally" bring his army buddies home to meet me.

James spoke about a friend of his often, insisting we would make the perfect couple, but he was unable to convince his friend to meet me. Jim was about James' age and when he found out that I was a lot younger than he was, he wanted nothing to do with meeting me. I was unsure about the meeting myself. I had never dated an older man and didn't know if I wanted to get involved with another soldier, who might have to leave at any moment.

As I was fixing dinner one night, the phone start to ring.

"Barbara, stop what you're doing, comb your hair and we'll pick you up in thirty minutes." Rose ordered from the other end of the receiver. "Jim has agreed to meet you and the four of us are going out tonight."

"I don't have a baby-sitter." I told her.

And I'd also like to know just what I was getting into. I felt like I was about to be on display for Jim's approval and wasn't quite sure if I wanted to go through with it.

"You can bring the boys to my house and my baby-sitter will watch them. You need a night out, and besides, what is there to lose? You have a nice dinner and never see each other again or you fall madly in love."

I doubted the latter would happen, but Rose was right, I needed a night out away from the boys, so I agreed to go with them. I quickly packed the boys' things and headed for my closet to find something to wear. It's been a long time since I bought any clothes for myself, so I had troubles finding something to wear on a date. I finally picked out a skirt and blouse and hoped it would do. I wished I had asked Rose what she was wearing so I could dress accordingly. Surely, she would have said if we were going someplace formal.

I told Rose I would wait outside at the corner for them to pick the boys and me up. I was nervous enough about this blind date and if it didn't work out, I didn't want Jim to know where I lived. With Allan in my arms, Brad holding my hand and balancing my purse and diaper bag over my shoulder, I took off to wait for Rose and James to pick me up.

Ten minutes later I heard a car approaching. James pulled next to me and got out to help me settle the boys into the car.

"Did they come alone?" I thought to myself. "Did Jim change his mind?"

At first, I didn't see anyone else in the car, so I was a little disappointed. Maybe they picked me up first. Rose put Brad in the front seat with her and then opened the back seat for me to get in. That's when I saw him. My date. Drunk, passed out and slouched over in the back seat of the car!

"What has James gotten me into? "I thought.

He said we would be a perfect match and he brings this person for me to meet. I couldn't stand drinking and he brings me a drunk date? I got in beside Jim, having to push him to his side. He wreaked of alcohol. We headed for Rose's to drop off the kids. We were supposed to go to dinner but how? Jim couldn't even sit up, let alone eat anything.

At the time I was furious but later we had many laughs about that first meeting.

"I'm sorry, Barbara." James apologized. "It wasn't supposed to be like this. Honest. Jim was so nervous about meeting you he asked to stop at a tavern first to loosen up. Whatever he ordered hit him hard! I have never seen him drink before."

I just glared at James. How could he let this happen? I could tell this would be a very unforgettable evening and I was already wishing it was over. James rolled Jim onto the sofa while Rose went to get some coffee.

"Maybe we can sober him up enough to eat so you can see the real guy behind this face." James said.

I sat in the rocking chair across from Jim, staring at the bum.

"Some impression I made on you." I thought to myself.

He didn't even know I was there. Even slouched over, I could tell he was about my height, but he weighed a lot less. I estimated his weight to be about one hundred and thirty pounds and I wondered if the man ever ate anything, as small as he was. James said he was a cook, but from the size of him, he didn't eat any of his own cooking. He had dark brown hair, cut short, and supported a pair of glasses on the tip of his nose, which looked like they were ready to fall off. He had a dark complexion making it appear like he spent more time in the sun than in a kitchen in front of the stove.

James and Rose were determined not to let this spoil my night and show me another side of Jim, the side they knew. Because they were my friends and I trusted their judgment, I decided to let them sober him up and start anew. A decision I will always be thankful for. Had I decided to walk away that day, there's no telling in which direction my life would have gone.

Rose came back with the coffee and started trying to pour some down Jim's throat while James dribbled ice water over his friend's head. I tried to hold back my laughter but the sight of this grown man being held up by his two friends, head dripping with water and coffee running down his chin, was more than I could take. Though I tried my hardest to be mad at the three of them, the laughter came. I laughed so hard and so long that they stopped their antics and stared at me like I was the one who was crazy.

Jim, who was sober by that time, soaking wet, glasses speckled with water and still slanted on his nose, just stared at me. He didn't understand why I was laughing. He looked at me with a strange expression as though he were thinking, "Who are you and why are you laughing at me?" If only he could have seen himself at that moment.

Jim sobered up and James was able to introduce the two of us properly.

"As soon as my buddy here dries himself off maybe we can finally go out to dinner." James said as he shoved his friend toward the bathroom.

A short while later, Jim emerged from the bathroom wearing fresh clothes, his hair combed, and his glasses sitting properly on his nose. He looked completely different than he did a short while before and I suddenly became awfully curious about this man. I knew at that moment that Jim would someday be an important part of my life.

Dinner that night was the start of a new adventure. As I sat next to Jim in the booth, I saw the way he stared at me. I knew he liked what he saw and just hoped it wasn't my imagination that I was seeing admiration in his eyes.

Jim hit it off instantly with the boys. Only two weeks after we met, he spoke of making a life with me and finally giving the boys a father.

"I don't normally rush into things but I'm in the army and could move out at any time. I'm on standby to go to Vietnam and would like you to be my wife before I must go. If we were married before that happens, you and the boys can get all the army has to offer to dependents. You would be taken care of for life. I know we have only known each other for two weeks but I already know that I want to share my life with you." He told me.

I was flabbergasted and didn't know what to say at the time. I didn't know him very well, but after all, Mom only knew my Dad for two weeks before they married, and they were happy. I knew I didn't, at that time love him, but love could come later. What he offered was a dream come true and I didn't only have myself to think about. I held Brad and Allan's futures in my hands. Could I deny them the security Jim offered and a father they so much needed?

There was one other problem that needed to be addressed, one that Jim was still unaware of. I couldn't marry him now because legally, I was still married to Lloyd. I couldn't save the money needed to file for a divorce. Until that moment, I had no reason to legally end my marriage.

"You have given me a lot to think about, Jim, however, it is a decision that I need to think about. I hope you can understand and wait for a day or two."

Jim looked at me with understanding in his eyes and gently took me in his arms for a tender kiss.

I didn't sleep much that night, trying to come to a decision that I could live with. I didn't love Jim the way he wanted me to, so I had to ask myself if it would be fair to marry him. But there were so many reasons why I should say yes to his proposal. The boys had already grown fond of Jim and he offered me a life away from welfare and scraping by. By the time morning came, I knew that I would say yes to Jim and I would grow to love him. Maybe, just maybe, I would grow to love him the way he should be loved.

When Jim came over that evening, I was ready to give him my answer. After the boys were in bed and we settled on the couch to watch television, I took his hand in mine and started talking.

"Jim, I have thought about your proposal and I want to say yes, but there is something you must know that may prevent us from marrying as soon as you want. I couldn't afford to get a divorce from my first husband and now I don't know what to do."

Jim kissed me and assured me that would not be a problem.

"I have some money saved and tomorrow we will go to the courthouse together to start proceedings."

As he promised, Jim took the day off from work and was at my door early the next morning to take me into town. Rose watched the boys and we headed to the courthouse. After filing the papers, the clerk told us that in three months, I would be single. Three months! We didn't realize it would take that long and didn't want to wait to get married, but what choice did we have.

"It will be okay honey; three months is not that long, and it will give you a chance to plan a wedding."

I knew he was right, but I was afraid that something would go wrong. What if he changed his mind or the army sent him away from me? As if the army heard my fears, they intervened with our plans. That same night, when Jim called me, he sounded very upset.

"I have bad news, Barbara. I'm on standby to leave for Vietnam. It could be a matter of hours or days before I must go. I don't want to leave you before we get married. There has to be a way to speed up the divorce."

I didn't know what we could do. I had this fear of Jim going to war and not coming back. I wanted to be his wife before he left so, we decided to get married anyway. Jim wanted me to be able to collect his checks while he was gone and to get the free medical care the army offered. The only way was to get married. The next day we drove to the next county and applied for a license, hoping that they wouldn't see that I wasn't yet legally divorced. It would take three days for the license to go through. We held our breath, hoping that the army would hold off calling Jim to war.

151

Three days later, dressed in a simple two-piece suit, I married Jim in the army chapel with only Rose and James present as witnesses. After the short ceremony, the four of us went to a nice restaurant for dinner and then I found myself alone with my new husband. We knew it was not a legal marriage, but we put our fears aside. This was my wedding night. I had another fear worse than not being legally married. Because of my past sexual experiences, I feared sex and I dreaded what I knew would be expected of me as Jim's wife. Jim would probably understand if he knew but I wanted to please him and after all maybe this time it would be different.

Jim was gently taking his time, slowly removing my clothes, exploring my body as he went. As he touched me, I stiffened up. I tried but I couldn't relax. And so, once again I pretended, hoping Jim wouldn't notice, and from the way he continued, I knew I pleased him. I would never tell him how I felt and maybe someday, I would no longer have to pretend.

The next day, Jim took me to get my military card and I was then an army wife. We knew if the army ever found out we weren't legally married, Jim would be reprimanded, if not kicked out, so we kept quiet.

One month passed, then two, without Jim getting orders. The boys loved having Jim there. He truly became their father, playing with them at night while I fixed dinner. We would tuck them into bed together and read them a goodnight story.

Jim decided it was time I learned how to drive and get a license before he had to leave me. The only time I ever sat behind the wheel was in driver's education in high school. At the end of the course, my teacher told me, "I will pass you if you promise never be on the road again!"

Until Jim came along, I decided it was best to listen to the teacher. It was unsafe to all involved if I ever operated a vehicle of any kind.

Jim was patient in teaching me. In a very short time I passed the test and became a licensed driver.

In the third month of our marriage, I received my divorce papers in the mail. It was final at last and now Jim and I could legally marry. That afternoon, we applied again for another license and in three days, we once again stood before a minister repeating our vows.

The second marriage was held at the Lutheran church I went to with Mom years ago. I wanted to be married in the Baptist church I now attended but because I was divorced, they wouldn't marry us. My dad and Rose stood by us as witnesses this time. I was very surprised that Dad agreed to come to my wedding. As far as he knew, this was my first wedding. He never knew that three months before I said these same vows to the same man beside me.

The day after our second marriage, Jim was suddenly sent to Vietnam without any warning. We only had six hours to pack his things and to say goodbye. We knew the day was coming but I was still not prepared. I was married but now I would once again be forced into living alone. I drove Jim to the army depot and kissed him goodbye, trying not to cry. I would not see him for a year, but he would be back. I had to tell myself that. Though I knew soldiers were getting killed over there every day, Jim would come home safely to me.

I heard from Jim often. In each letter, he told me over and over how much he loved me. Along with each letter he sent me pictures of his camp, his army buddies, their army mascot, never mentioning the danger he was in. He made it sound as if he was away at summer camp for boys, having the time of his life. But we both knew without putting into words the danger he was in. I prayed to God each night to bring him safely home to me.

The weeks turned into month's and the marks on my calendar were filling up. I busied myself learning to be a good wife to Jim. I practiced cooking good meals, sewing the boys' clothes and decorating the house. I missed Jim terribly, but I knew that as an army wife, this was to be the first of many separations and I had to get used to being alone.

Jim fell in love with me despite the size of my body. He never indicated that he was displeased with how I looked, but I was unhappy with having to wear size eighteen clothes. I wanted to wear swimming suits without embarrassment. I wanted to give Jim something in return for the love he gave me, so while he was gone, I decided to try to lose some weight, and make him proud of me.

While at the store one day, I found an advertisement of a weight loss group held weekly at a nearby church. Free daycare was even offered. So, I had no excuses not to attend. I was used to doing things alone, so when the meeting day came, I bundled the kids up and drove the three blocks to the church.

TOPS (Take Off Pounds Sensibly) became my second home the year Jim was gone. The members made me feel at home. I didn't feel like a "nothing." I had friends at last, friends who didn't care what I looked like or how big I was. Friends without questions, reaching out their hands too me and welcoming me into their group.

Brad and Allan made friends with the other kids in the daycare and looked forward to going to TOPS as much as I did. The weekly contest and incentives to help us lose weight were fun, but each week I became discouraged because no matter how much I dieted, I was not losing weight. I did not give up though because whether I lost or gained weight, I enjoyed the meetings and having an hour away from my boys was a godsend while I waited for Jim's return home.

Chapter 18

Military life

1967

I don't know what it was about Jim that Dad liked but somehow, I believe he approved of him because he was an army career man like himself and because he was so much older than I was. Maybe he thought Jim would be able to control me the way Dad wanted to. I wasn't ready for Jim to leave me, especially right after we were married. He didn't want to leave any more than I wanted him to go.

The year flew by faster than I anticipated and before I knew it, Jim was back from Vietnam and we continued where we left off. The boys didn't remember him at first and were shy. They drew back when he reached his arms out to them, but after a while, Jim had warmed up to them and was soon wrestling with both boys on the floor once again.

Money was tight and trying to support two boys on Jim's army pay was tough, but we did it together. I even got used to constantly moving from post to post. I didn't complain, remembering all those times Mom, Jackie and I had to do the same every time Dad was reassigned. We had to pull up stakes, leave our friends and move the boys away from a home they were getting used to. I hated to leave my friends, but I made new ones. I was excited to see places I only read about before.

Fort Ord, California

Jim was first assigned to go to California two short months after coming home. I loved the weather and made some good friends. I got involved with a group of other wives from the post that came together once a week to visit the VA hospital, volunteer at the Red Cross and put together care packages for new families in the area. We were there for a little over a year when Jim got orders for Korea and once again, I was faced with him leaving me.

There were two distinct memories I had during my time in California. They both involve Brad.

The first one resulted in the first of many apologies I would have to make regarding his behavior. Brad decided that shoplifting was a fun thing to do. One day I discovered candy and small toys in his pockets. After questioning him, he admitted to taking the items from the grocery store when we were there the last time. I took his hand, along with the things that he took, back to the store. We faced the manager together. With tears in his eyes, he was made to apologize. I thought that would be enough to scare him from doing it again, but it turned into a habit. We made that trip with the same apology more than once.

The second biggest memory of that time was when Brad discovered girls…at the age of four!

He made friends with a girl named Sharon who was also four. The two of them played together every day, either at our house or at Sharon's. One day, I called Brad to lunch and could not find him anywhere. I thought I heard giggling from Brad's room but when I looked, no one was there. I could still hear the giggling which sounded like it was coming from the closet. I opened the door and there sat Sharon and Brad stark naked, laughing at being caught.

Moses Lake, Washington

We of course couldn't go when Jim was assigned to go to Korea, so the boys and I got an assignment of our own. The army offered me and the boys housing in Moses Lake Washington. A place that use to be an army post but was now closed and housed the wives of servicemen who were overseas. So, we headed there. After we were settled in, we exchanged tearful goodbyes. Before I knew it, Jim was gone. I was once again alone. The apartment was nice, and we had a small yard for the boys to play in. There were neighbors on both sides of us. It seemed like one big family. The neighbors were all the same as us, with children and a husband who was gone, stationed somewhere overseas. We all formed a special bond, getting together as much as we could. Brad was about five and Allan was three at the time, so my days were full chasing after two rambunctious boys.

I could tell even then; Brad was going to be my problem child. I couldn't take my eyes off him for a second before he'd be into something. Sometimes he'd leave the yard and I had to search for him while watching Allan at the same time. Brad made friends with a neighbor boy about his age and they were together all the time.

One day I called for Brad and started one of my many searches for him. As I started out the door, I spot Brad, head down, slowly walking home. As he came closer, I could see his clothes were filthy, covered in white dust and grease on his pants. He looked up at me, with tears in his eyes, knowing he might be in trouble.

158

"What happened?" I asked.

"I was just playing with David, Mommy!"

I took him straight to the bathroom to change his clothes and make him take a bath. As he was in the tub I looked more closely at his clothes and sniffed the powder.

"That's flour." I said aloud wondering how he could have gotten into that.

Soon the doorbell rang. I went to answer the door and found David's mother standing there. She was holding David by the arm in one hand and clutching his dirty shirt in the other, shaking it at me.

"Did you notice any difference in Brad?" She asked. "I think our boys have been up to no good".

I forgot I still had Brad's pants still in my hand and I held them up in the same manner.

"I think whatever it was they did it together..." Then she paused. The irony of both of us standing there, holding up their greasy, floured clothes caused us both to start laughing.

We knew that eventually we'd have to question the boys. With both of us standing there, facing each other, with the evidence in our hands was too much. When the laughter subsided, I asked her in and called in Brad who was now out of the bath, and into some clean clothes.

David and Brad sat close together on the couch staring at us.

David's mother was the first to speak. "OK boys. It's time to tell us where you've been and what you've been doing."

Brad spoke first. "I'm sorry Mommy. We were visiting the neighbor's house and sort of got into things… then he started crying.

"Are you saying you were next door? They're at work? Who was there to let you in?" I asked with a louder voice that was intended.

"We climbed through the doggy door. We just wanted to pet the doggy." David said.

So, with boys in tow and Allan following close behind, the five of us headed next door to evaluate the situation. The back door was wide open, confirming the boy's presence and their escape route. We entered the house and couldn't believe that two little boys made such a big mess.

There was flour in every corner of the kitchen, on the countertops and covering the stove. An empty bag of sugar lay on the floor with the contents dumped and footprints carved into the sugar mound. An empty carton of eggs sat on the counter with broken eggs spread over the counters and on the floor, mixed in with the flour. Peanut butter was finger painted on the walls and shortening covered the doors and refrigerator. We were silent as we examined the damage. I was too afraid to speak. Afraid I would lash out at Brad, words that cannot be taken back.

David's mom went home to get mops, buckets, rags and soap while I started picking up the empty containers. It took us four hours that day to clean up the mess, making the boys help. It was clean but not perfect. There were cabinet knobs broken, and scratches on the linoleum. We left the neighbor a note explaining what had happened and asked her to send us a bill for the damage. We then locked up her house and took the boys home.

The next day I made Brad go over to apologize, another of the many apologies he had to make to various people throughout his younger years.

Columbus, Georgia

Jim returned home from Korea and received his new orders. This time, we were to move to Georgia.

On the way to our new home we decided to take our time and do a little sightseeing. Jim had been gone for a while. He had a month before reporting to his new assignment in Columbus, Georgia. We needed this time for fun and to allow Jim to try to bond with the boys.

The scenery we passed was beautiful. It was summer and it was hot. The boys were fidgeting and fighting in the back seat. We tried to make many stops to cool off and stretch our legs and let the boys run. I remember one stop vividly. It was when we entered New Mexico and Jim decided to make a stop at the famous Carlsbad Caverns. I read a lot about the caverns and have always wanted to go so I was as excited as the kids.

The place was crowded with tourists. Jim and I had a boy each by the hand, making them stay close so they would not get lost. The caverns were beautiful! As we went further down underground, I was amazed at the rock formation, the color, and the sound of the boy's voices echoing back off the walls of the caves.

Somehow Brad got loose from my grip and wandered off. One minute he was there and the next he wasn't. I called for him but all I heard was my voice echoing back. We asked some of the other people on the tour, but no one had seen him. The tour guide phoned security to help look and asked for us to wait by the entrance. They didn't want me wandering off and getting lost too. Also, there were many places you could fall. I frantically waited and waited. About twenty minutes later, a guard returned with Brad in tow, grinning and ready to tell me about his adventure.

He saw a bat high above and wanted to catch him, so he ran ahead, unaware of all the dangers around.

We wanted to finish the tour since it was almost over, but after the scare with Brad, my heart wasn't in it.

Once we exited the caves, I decided I wanted a souvenir, so we entered the shop. An older lady was behind the register ringing up customers. I found what I wanted immediately, a coffee cup to ad to my collection. By the time we were ready to check out, the customers were all gone, and we were alone in the store. We were on our way out when the lady yelled...

"STOP!"

Before we knew what was going on, she had Brad by the collar, yelling at him and shaking him. He was loudly wailing and yelling for me.

"He has something of ours in his pocket! Little thief!" She yelled.

Jim stepped in and gently grabbed Brad away from the clerk

"Brad what is in your pocket?" He asked

Wiping his tears away with his sleeve, he pulled out two rocks that were from the caverns. The one thing that would be appealing to young boys. Jim made Brad apologize to the lady. We turned to leave when the lady

162

again grabbed Brad, yelling at him and shaking him once again.

"It's wrong! No one steals from me!"

I saw the look in Jim's face when he turned around.

"Lady I don't know who you think you are. He's just a little boy and he said he's sorry. Let him go, now!" he yelled back.

With that, Jim swung his arm out and punched the lady. My mouth dropped open as I have never seen Jim even raise his voice before.

"No one treats my son like that." And we were out the door.

We jumped in our car and we were off. I've never seen Jim drive so fast, but we just knew that by now, the police would be called, and we were now wanted fugitives. Or so I thought. I hung on silently praying. Allan was crying, not knowing what happened but Mom was upset and that was all he needed to know. To Brad, it was an adventure and was clapping and cheering yelling, "Police!" I wasn't sure if he knew exactly what he did or what Jim did to protect him. It was just a game to him. We flew through New Mexico, frantically trying to get to the state line. I just knew I'd hear sirens at any time, if not for what happened at the caverns, then for speeding. I was scared but as Jim drove and we left New Mexico I relaxed and smiled. It was another Brad escapade, but I just now realized that when Jim yelled at that lady, he said, "My son". Jim had finally bonded with the boys and thought of them as his own.

We finally made it to our new home in Georgia. I loved the south. Things were so different there. It was hotter there than it was in California and the air conditioners were running nonstop. Though the summers were sweltering, the winters were unbearably cold. We were homebound for several weeks because the snow was so deep. The boys loved the snow. I hated it. I couldn't drive in it and was cooped up with two hyperactive kid's twenty-four hours a day.

Chapter 19

Georgia

1968

Another beautiful town, another home, new friends and faces. It was getting to be a routine by now. The kids were excited, especially Brad since he was finally getting to start school. He was almost six. It's time for a teacher to deal with his problems for a few hours a day and for me to get a few hours of rest. It was going to be just me and Allan during the day. Allan gave me very few problems. When he was up to something, he was following Brad's lead.

I decided to get a job to help with expenses. I thought it would keep me busy with Jim at work and Brad at school. With just Allan at home, it was getting lonely. I didn't know many people and thought this would be my chance to make some friends. A neighbor agreed to watch Allan when I found a job at a local pharmacy. I served customers hot dogs, milkshakes, and cashiered. I was tired when I got home and wanted some quiet time to myself, but Brad would be home from school waiting and dreaming up more ways to get into trouble.

Brad's first fascination with fire was in Georgia. I was at work that day and Jim was home with the boys. They were in their room playing and Jim was on the couch watching television. When I returned from work the house smelled smoky and I was told what happened.

Jim smelled something burning and started searching the house. Smoke was coming from the boy's room. He found Brad standing in the middle of the room. Allan was hiding under the covers of his bed. Under

Brad's bed was all his clothes in a pile burning. Brad decided he didn't like the clothes I bought him, so he decided to burn them up, using a lighter he found in the kitchen. The bed snuffed out the flames so the only damage, besides his clothes, was the charred mattress. The part that bothered me the most is what Jim told me of our son's behavior. He stood there smiling through the whole ordeal seeming to enjoy watching the fire, not realizing what he did was wrong.

We were only in Georgia for six months when Jim got orders once again. This time to Greece. Another assignment in which his family couldn't go with him. I was still having problems adjusting to military life, basically still being a newlywed. I was married now for over two years but in that time, Jim has gone to Viet Nam for a year, Korea and now Greece.

I was to remain behind to take care of things at home. We waited for the final orders, knowing it was coming soon. Two months later, he was gone.

Two months after Jim left, the phone rang. I got a bad feeling, chills running up my spine, not sure why I would react in such a way. I reached to answer it, turning the volume down on the television so I could hear who was on the other end.

"Honey, it's me." Jim was on the other end of the line, but he didn't sound like himself. I immediately became frightened because Jim wouldn't be calling me from Greece unless something was wrong. "Honey, please don't be alarmed but I wanted to be the one to tell you. During a routine physical yesterday, the doctors found a lump and I was sent to Walter Reed Hospital to have it checked out."

I wanted to go to him, but how? Brad was in school. There was no housing available and we did not have the money for me to travel. Jim was back in the states but still beyond my reach. We talked for a while. More like he did most of the talking, trying to comfort me and assure me that he was feeling okay. Jim hung up after promising he would keep me informed. I found myself praying to God that the lump would turn out to be nothing and we would have worried needlessly.

Two days later, the doctor from Walter Reed called me and I knew that my prayers went unanswered. If there was nothing wrong Jim would have called me, not his doctor.

"I'm sorry but I wanted to be the one to tell you about your husbands' condition. We did some testing on the lump and I am sorry to be the one to tell you, but Jim does have cancer in his left testicle and surgery is scheduled for tomorrow to have it removed."

I wanted to cry but I was not one to show my emotions to strangers, so I kept quiet. There were so many questions I wanted to ask. Most of all, I wanted to be there. I didn't want Jim to go through this alone. We couldn't afford the plane ticket for me to go be with him, so I had to stay behind. The waiting was unbearable as I sat by the phone, hoping for word on the surgery.

Jim made it through just fine but had a lot of rehabilitating to do, so they kept him at the hospital for eleven months. We talked on the phone often, wrote letters and counted the days when he would come home. The question that was in my mind often (but I was afraid to ask Jim or his doctors) was, would that effect our sex life or his ability to have children. Those questions would wait until I could see Jim and ask him in person. I didn't want to discuss it over the phone.

Jim seemed his old self when he finally did come home. The rest and therapy at the hospital seemed to do

167

him a world of good. By looking at his outward appearance, you wouldn't have known how sick he was or what he had been through. The night Jim returned answered my first question; he could still perform as well as he did before. Though I didn't love Jim when I married him, I grew to love my husband more and more every day, but I still found myself pretending to enjoy the sex we shared.

The second question was answered for me by Jim's doctor two weeks after he returned home. Jim couldn't have a child of his own. We both talked about having one together and I never tried to prevent getting pregnant, but for some reason I never did. Now any chance we did have was gone.

Shortly after Jim came home, we were again uprooted and sent on our way to Massachusetts.

Chapter 20

Ayer, Massachusetts

1970-1972

Massachusetts was very similar to Georgia in both the weather and the scenery. The summers were hot and humid, the winters bitterly cold. The snow was several feet deep and remained on the ground for most of the winter keeping you trapped in your home. Ayer, Massachusetts was situated just outside the gate of Fort Devens army post, where Jim would be stationed next.

I loved the summers but wasn't too fond of the snow in the wintertime. I couldn't drive in it and hated not being able to get out of the house. The boys loved the snow; however. Allan was able to start kindergarten and by then, Brad was in the second grade. The state was used to the snow and rarely called off school because of it.

To my knowledge, Massachusetts was the first and probably the only state that Brad behaved himself in. No incidence to report, no police at our doors, no fires or complaining neighbors. Fingers crossed; maybe my son is growing up.

The only incident that comes to mind involving the boys was a dispute with our neighbor. That day the boys were in their squabbling mood. Fighting, yelling, Screaming, and of course, Mom and Dad yelling at them to be quiet! The neighbors were entertaining, drinking mostly. We lived in a duplex. Our neighbors lived on the right side of us. The boys were trying to outdo the noise of the party next door. The man of the house had enough and started banging loudly on our door, yelling for the boys to "Shut Up!" Suddenly, he slammed his fist through our window. Glass shattered everywhere. MPs were called and the neighbor was taken off to jail. We boarded up the window and the boys stopped fighting, staring and laughing at the grownups. Things went back to normal, for the most part.

We were there for only two months when Jim brought up the subject of adoption. He wanted to adopt the boys and make them legally his. I had no idea he was even thinking about it. There were times I secretly had hoped we could truly become a family. I wanted so badly for the boys to one day take Jim's name. I ever knew how to bring it up, so to have Jim come up with the idea on his own meant a lot to me.   I think it was a combination of his near brush with death and not being able to have children of his own. For whatever reason I was not going to question it.

We visited with a lawyer and started proceedings. The law required publishing the adoption in the paper for two weeks to give the biological fathers a chance to come forward to object. I wasn't worried. I was across the country from where I assumed Lloyd or Syd lived so I doubted they would ever read a Massachusetts paper.

After two weeks, we set a court date. The big day came, the boys dressed in fancy suits, hair combed and stood in front of the judge. They each asked what they thought of Jim becoming their father and it was over. It only took a month for the courts to finalize the adoption and Jim was at last, a true father to the boys.

The boys were both in school and Jim was at work, so to keep from getting bored, I got a job at the neighborhood doughnut shop one block from our home. I could walk there, and the hours were perfect because I worked only while the boys were in school and in a small way, I felt like I was contributing something to the household finances.

I decided one day after work to stop by a nearby beauty salon. I sat under the hair dryer reading a magazine when an article caught my eye. The title of it was, "When the doctors say your husband can't have children."

It was an article about artificial insemination. I had heard about it before but never realized how many women out there had undergone the procedure, only to have beautiful babies nine months later. I doubted if Jim would be interested in the article, but it wouldn't hurt to show him.

I loved my boys dearly, but I longed for a daughter to cuddle and dress in fancy dresses. I realized that there would be no guarantee I would not have another boy but regardless, I would love another child no matter what the sex, but would Jim be as excited as I was?

After dinner that night, I cuddled next to Jim and showed him the article.

"Honey, I want to show you an article I read today." I told him.

Jim had three brothers who each had children. They were always asking him when he was going to follow suit and have children of his own. Jim could not bring himself to admit to his brothers that he was unable to. He never told them about the cancer and his infertility so he led them to believe that someday it would happen. It was because of that, Jim agreed to check into the procedure.

"Sounds interesting. Do you think we should look into it?" he said to my surprise.

He wanted another child as much as I did, and his brothers would never have to know that biologically, it wasn't his.

"It wouldn't hurt anything to ask my doctor next time I see him."

On my next visit to my gynecologist, I brought up the subject and asked if they had done artificial inseminations at their hospital.

"It's a long process and I'd need to talk to your husband first, to see if it's really what you both want." He told me.

Before I knew what was happening, the doctor was making me an appointment to start the process. He seemed more excited than we were about proceeding as if I were his first patient to go through with the procedure.

I was handed thermometers, charts, graphs and literature to read while I waited. Morning and night, I was told to take my temperature. If I forgot, Jim was there holding the thermometer.

Jim was tested and his physical description noted because as we were told they would try to get a donor who matched the characteristics of both of us.

When it was closer to insemination time, the hospital ordered the semen from a Boston hospital. It was almost like ordering something from a catalog.

I was instructed to take my temperature daily and note it on a graph. When my temperature hit a certain high, I was to come in immediately. It took two months to find the perfect day and we were getting discouraged. It seemed like it shouldn't take this long. Finally, the perfect day came, the thermometer rose, and I eagerly called Jim

"I think it's time, can you pick me up and get me to the doctor as soon as you can?"

You would have thought I was in labor and going to give birth the way the two of us acted.

The hospital had the donor's sperm sent to them and before I could change my mind, it was done. It only took a few minutes. I held Jim's hand while the doctor inserted the semen. I was instructed to lay there, feet in stirrups for an hour. During that time, we made plans and talked names for our baby. We were sure this would take. We would be so disappointed if it didn't.

There was nothing left to do but wait to see if I was pregnant. In my heart, I already knew that I was. I missed my next period and had the answer we were waiting for. We were going to have a baby.

I was three months pregnant when Jim sprang the news on me. In three months, he was due to retire, and he had his choice where he wanted to settle. Jim knew how much I wanted to return to Washington. We were going home! I would be due in six months, Jim would be out of the army, and our baby would be born in Tacoma! No more moving around! We could at last make a home for the kids, a home we would not have to leave.

Chapter 21

Tacoma, Washington

1972

A week before Christmas, we pulled into Dad's driveway. I didn't want to stay with him, but we really couldn't afford a hotel and had nowhere else to go. I was hoping that it would be a short-term solution, especially since it was so crowded. As soon as we could, we would find a place to live.

It wasn't as bad as I thought it would be. Dad liked Jim and he seemed to be excepting me, treating me better than he ever had since Mom died. Gail didn't say too much while we were there. I had the feeling from her expressions that she would rather we weren't like we were intruding on their life. I tried to stay out of her way as much as possible, trying to keep the boys quiet and out of her way.

We spent a lot of time house hunting. With help from the government we were able to get a loan and found a beautiful home, located on a dead-end street just a couple blocks from the school. The house had three bedrooms, one and a half bathrooms, a fireplace and a nice fenced yard. At last, I had a home of my own! No landlords to deal with. The boys could walk to school. We moved in a week later.

Jim started his new job at a steakhouse in town as a cook. I started decorating our home and getting involved in school activities. Brad joined the Boy Scouts and made a few friends. We were finally a part of a community. I started fixing up one of the bedrooms into a nursery.

My pregnancy was a lot easier than I remembered it being with the boys. I never had morning sickness and gained very little weight. Jim and I spent our free time shopping for baby items.

Two o'clock in the afternoon on June fifth, I started labor. At least I thought it was labor. I had one huge contraction and waited, but no more pains came. Jim was home that day and the boys had just come in from school. We didn't want to take any chances, so we loaded the boys into the car in order to drop them off at the designated sitters and headed to the hospital. We entered the emergency room at four o'clock and Jim was whisked away to fill out the admitting papers. I got into a hospital gown and my doctor came in to see me. Before I knew it, I was in the delivery room and my baby was coming. There was time to give me anything for pain or to prepare me for delivery. By the time Jim came back, at four-fifteen, our baby daughter was born, fifteen minutes after we arrived at the hospital.

We decided from the start, if we had a girl, we would name her Angela Hope. Throughout my pregnancy, Jim would often pat my belly and make comments such as, "How is hopeless doing?" and "How are you and No Hope?" He thought he was being funny, but I wondered is his teasing would end at the birth. Before he arrived after finishing the paperwork, I asked the nurse if I could start filling out the birth certificate. I started to fill in Angela for her first name. When I got to her second name, I thought frantically if this is the name she should have for the rest of her life. If her Daddy teases her, would others? I loved the name because after all I've been through, this baby girl gave me hope for a better life. I put the pen to the paper and wrote the first name I thought of…Ranae. I didn't know the correct way to spell it but who cares. It would be original if it's wrong. Jim arrived and asked how Angel

Hope is doing? "About that…" I said and showed him the birth certificate. I was afraid he would get mad that I changed her name without discussing it with him first. He read the name out loud, "Angela Ranae." And said, "I love it. Her daddy called her Angel from the first day of her life. She was our pride and joy and we never once regretted the decision to have her.

I knew the boys wished for another brother, but after they inspected their new baby sister, they decided she'd do. They wanted to help care for her from the first day we brought her home, even attempting to help change her diaper, but that phase didn't last for more than two days. They realized diaper changing was overrated. Brad then thought he could help feed her, but Angel decided to spit up on him and that was it. From then on, they decided the care of the baby should be my responsibility.

I couldn't have asked for a more perfect baby. Angel slept through the night from the beginning and rarely cried. Jim adored his daughter. Except for when he was at work, the two of them were never apart. While she was still a baby, he would push her in the stroller through the malls, enjoying the attention strangers would give to his Angel. As she got older, he would teach her how to throw a ball, and when she was only two, he took her to the lake for her first fishing lesson. There were times when I felt left out of their activities. It was father and daughter most of the time while I stayed home with the boys. I'm sure if I asked, I probably would've been welcome on their journeys, but I didn't want to interfere. I was jealous. Not because of their relationship, but because Angel had something with her dad that I never had, and always wanted with my own dad.

Jim wasn't happy at the house we'd bought and talked about moving. We started having problems with our next-door neighbors. I loved that house and for sentimental reasons, I didn't want to leave it. It was our first house together and where we took Angel home for the first time. I had hoped we'd stay there forever but Jim was displeased with the neighbors on both sides of us. On one side, the couple had two dogs that constantly barked. After Jim approached them about the noise, they made it unbearable for us to be outdoors when they were. They shouted snide comments at as and threw trash into our yard. The problem we had with the other neighbor was their children. They were about the same age as our boys. They would use foul language and we caught them once trying to get Brad to share a cigarette. Jim did not want the boys around that environment, so we moved.

Our new house wasn't nearly as nice as the one we moved from, but it had a huge front yard to keep the kids in and neighbors who weren't as close as our last ones were. The house badly needed repairs, which we had hoped to do someday. The one thing I loved was the dozen fruit trees in our yard, each blooming with fruit. The boys would have to change schools, but their new school was only a block away.

From the outside, the house appeared to be larger than it was. The front room was small with a wood burning stove in the corner. The kitchen was larger than the rest of the downstairs put together. The only bedroom downstairs could only fit a bed and dresser, the laundry room was on the back porch. The room upstairs was an open space without closets and there was a small room off in one corner. We'd decided to let the boys have the larger room and hang a curtain across the smaller room for Angel.

Jim loved the house and his excitement over remodeling soon caught on. Together we'd make plans on just how we would improve our home some day when we could afford it, but it was only a dream the two of us shared. We never had the time or the money to make it happen.

Chapter 22

Goodbye Jim

1977

The end of October, Jim started complaining about his back hurting and I was starting to get worried. He wasn't one to complain so I had a feeling it was worse than he was letting on. I caught him soaking in hot baths of water several times a day, and he would call in sick to work several times a week until his boss told him to take some time off. I finally convinced Jim to see a doctor and after a few tests, he was admitted to the hospital.

In five days, Jim's condition went from bad to worse and the doctors still couldn't figure out what was wrong with him. I spent every waking hour with my husband, wishing I could share his pain. Brad, who was now fifteen years old, and Allan, at twelve, was able to manage things at home and take care of their sister who was now four.

A week had passed by without knowing what was wrong with him. It was agonizing waiting for answers until the day finally arrived that I would learn Jim's fate. The doctor called me into his office to tell me the news. "Jim has a rare cancer in the lining of his heart. It would only be a matter of time. All we can do now is keep him comfortable."

"There has to be something that can be done. Cancer is cured every day. Jim has beat cancer before and I know he can do it again." I insisted.

But the look on the doctor's face told me differently. "He shouldn't be in any pain." He said. Then the doctor told me what Jim said.

"He told me not to be alarmed that you would take it so well. He said you're a private person and will wait till you are at home in your room to cry in private. Can I sill get someone for you to talk to?"

Jim knew me so well. I didn't realize just how much. People think of me sometimes as uncaring because I don't show my emotions. I think it comes from years of being hurt and trying to seem tough. I never wanted others to know how bad things got to me.

I told the doctor, "No, that's ok. Jim was right. I just need to be alone."

That night I went home, closed the bedroom door and cried for what seemed like hours, till there were no tears left.

Normally the hospital wouldn't allow children but because Jim was terminal, they made an exception. That night I brought the kids to see their dad. The boys had never been around anyone who was sick before, so they didn't know what to expect. They cowered in the corner with wide frightening eyes. Angel, in her four-year old innocence, thought her daddy was just sleeping and crawled upon his bed. She laid her head on his chest. Jim struggled to raise his arm and drew it around his daughter, pulling her closer to him. He would never see Angel grow up, graduate from high school, or give her away on her wedding day. At the sight of them, I could hold back the tears no longer. My one wish was that Angel would remember her daddy, but young minds forget, and I knew the day would come when she would have no recollection of him.

Christmas, 1977, was spent in Jim's room. The hospital cafeteria sent us Christmas dinner and tried to make us as comfortable as they could. By then, Jim was in a semi coma. He couldn't talk but his eyes were open, and the doctors said he knew I was there and could hear me. I sat beside his bed and read to him the many cards we received, and I quietly played Christmas music on the radio. Angel drew a card and laid it on his bed, hoping her daddy would read it when he woke up.

The only time I went home was to eat, shower and change clothes. I was beat but I was afraid to be away from Jim too long at a time. I did not want him to be alone in the end, but the doctor insisted I go home.

"There's nothing you can do for him now. You need some sleep and your children will need your strength afterwards."

He was right and so on December thirty-first; I went home to be with my children even though I sensed that I wouldn't see Jim again. I kissed him for what I knew was the last time and walked away, not looking back.

That evening at eleven o-clock, the doctor called me to tell me Jim was gone. I dropped the phone as if it burned me and stared at it. The phone woke the boys and Brad came to me knowing from my reaction what had happened. He put his arms around me and soothed me as if I was the child and he was the parent. January first, 1978 was Allan's thirteenth birthday. We should have been celebrating his becoming a teenager, but instead, I was planning a funeral and notifying family.

It was a beautiful funeral. Jim had a lot of friends and the chapel was filled. I didn't want to bring Angel because she didn't understand what was happening. Everyone thought she belonged with us, so I dressed her in her daddy's favorite dress, and she sat quietly beside me at the service. Songs were sung and friends of Jim's rose to speak of how kind and generous he was. Friends from work that I never met before. The casket was opened at the end of the service so the guests could form a line to say goodbye to their friend. I chose to be the last because I wanted extra time to wish my love a safe journey. Unsure of what to do, the boys quickly passed by their dad to steal a quick glance. Angel took my hand and together we walked forward. I wasn't sure how Angel would react but what she did shocked us all. As little as she was, she raised herself up onto the casket so she could see her Dad and reached for a nearby rosebud. She reached over to him and placed the rose on his chest and said,

"Wake up Daddy, I got you a flower. Wake up! I love you." Then she looked up at me with a tear running down her cheek. There was not a dry eye in the room.

Chapter 23

California, Here I Come

1978

The weeks and months after Jim died were lonely. For twelve years I had someone who cared about me and took care of me but suddenly, I was once again alone. Alone to make decisions that once were shared with Jim.

Financially I could make it, thanks to Jim's retirement check, but I had my doubts if I could go on emotionally. For my children, I knew I had to try. I had them to think about and for the moment couldn't consider my own needs.

While Jim was alive, besides the children, he was all I needed. He was my lover, my friend, and the father I never had in my own dad. He was my confidant and my soul mate. We were as one and I was more content then I had been in a long time, so when he died, I lost more than a husband whom I loved dearly. I lost my best friend, and I found myself once again isolated.

I was lost after Jim died. Having my children around was of some comfort but they had lives and friends of their own. I could not expect them to be with me all the time.

Jim's insurance came through and for the first time in my life, I had money. Jim's final bills were paid. His funeral expenses were taken care of which gave me a few thousand dollars left over. In my heart, I knew I should save the money for our future, but I was like a kid in a candy store. I bought clothes for the kids and myself, bought new furniture and took the vacation I had away dreamed of.

I needed to get away from Tacoma for just a little while, so I packed up Allan and Angel, jumped in the car and took off for California. Unfortunately, Brad was in Echo Glen and couldn't join us (which will be explained later in my story). I knew the trip wouldn't be easy. I'd never driven that far before, and the kids were too young to be of much help.

I wrote my friends in Oregon and California, planning short visits with each. We were in no hurry to get to our destination and in no hurry to come home, so we took our time. We drove only a few hours a day, stopping to sightsee along the way, and camping at rest areas when I was tired.

I drove along the Oregon coast and it was absolutely beautiful. The kids, much to my surprise, were getting along and gave me no problems at all. Driving with the Pacific Ocean in view and listening to the radio, brought me the peace I haven't had in a long time. Allan, at age thirteen, helped me spot road signs and kept the map within easy reach. We played games and sang, having the time of our lives.

It took me a little over a week to enter California. My first stop was at my sister, Jackie's. Jackie had a job and couldn't get the time off, so we were left to entertain ourselves while we were there. I probably saw my sister a total of six hours in the three days I stayed with her.

On the second day at Jackie's, the kids and I drove the ten miles to my old home, Jolon. I was anxious to see the old place and had hoped my childhood friend, Ronnie, was still there.

"Would he still remember me?" I wondered.

I stopped in front of the sign that said, "Welcome to Jolon", but that was all that remained of the little town I remembered. The general store was no longer there, replaced by a larger grocery store. The trailer park was still there but it was bare of trailers. I stared at the store and could see Ronnie and myself as children, running out of the store, happily playing our childish games. Maybe I would recognize someone, at least I hoped I would, but they were all strangers. I let the kids pick out a bottle of soda and a candy bar and went to the cashier to pay for our purchase. I asked the girl behind the counter if she had heard of Ronnie or his family.

"I'm sorry, but in the five years I've owned this place, I don't recall the name." She said.

I was looking forward to coming home. Coming back to the place where Mom was happy. Back to the childhood I remembered. But everything had changed. Wherever Ronnie was, I hoped he was happy. I wondered if he ever thought about me and those long-ago years of our youth.

After we left Jackie's, we headed for Los Angeles. I promised the kid's a trip to Disneyland and I had a pen pal there who invited us to stay with them. On the way, we stopped at Marine land for a day with the dolphins.

Once in Los Angeles, I quickly found Jenny's house. Though we had written several letters, I was nervous about our first meeting, but she made me feel like family from the moment I pulled up to her house.

I wanted the kids to have fun, and like me, they needed to unwind. They had been through a lot in their short lives. With this trip, I was hoping to make it up to them.

We spent one glorious day at Disneyland and another day at Universal Studios. Jenny drove us to all the places she thought we'd like to see. Allan had fun

185

matching his feet to those of the stars on Hollywood Boulevard, and I enjoyed the tour of the star's homes. We took dozens of pictures to remember our vacation, but like the saying goes, all good things must come to an end. It was time to go home. I was running out of money and knew it was time to face reality and learn how to start over without Jim.

Chapter 24

Home at Last

1978

I still had my friends in my TOPS group and owed them a great deal of thanks for the support they gave me, both during Jim's illness and those months afterwards when things looked bleak and I was ready to give up. But their phone calls eventually stopped as well as their visits and I was once again alone. Sure, I had my children with me, but I longed to have Jim's arms around me, needing his love and companionship.

Shortly after returning from our vacation, I jumped full force into outside activities. Anything to keep me from facing the four walls at home, and the lonely nights surrounded by my memories. I joined Parents Without Partners. Some people didn't understand why I would join a singles group so soon after Jim's passing. Some thought I was being disloyal to him and that if I truly loved him, I would have grieved longer than I did. What those people didn't know was that I grieved alone at night with the lights out in silence. In my heart, I knew that Jim understood what I needed and that I would take the time to mourn in my own way, in private. I didn't need anybody in else in my life telling me how to grieve and for how long.

I did not join the group in hopes to meet a man. It was a once in a lifetime chance that I met and eventually fell in love with Jim. My past experiences with men prevented me from wanting one in my life so I doubted I'd be able to find that kind of love twice. I wasn't ready to get involved with anyone and I'm not sure I ever will again. Outsiders insisted I was on a hunt for a replacement for Jim. If only they knew. The only reason I joined the group

187

was because of my children, and for the support I would get from other mothers who understood what I was going through.

Every night, there were group discussions, from raising children to money matters. I went to every meeting I could get myself to. And there were always activities for the children. They made friends and were happier than I'd seen them in a long time.

I attended a few of the adult dances but I felt out of place. Though I made friends with the women, the men shied away from me, seldom asking me to dance. I felt I was once again the wallflower from high school, waiting, hoping for someone to notice me.

At the time I decided to become more active in the group activities, I started having severe abdominal pains. At first, I contributed it to my hectic schedule. I was always busy, on the run, grabbing a bite to eat when I had time, sleeping only when necessary. I wanted to avoid sleep as much as I could because of the dreams I would have, the empty place in my bed, and the silence of not hearing Jim's snoring next to me.

I spent a lot of time in the bathroom buckled over in pain, unable to breath. It was worse than any other I have felt in my life. I don't remember childbirth causing so much pain. I went to the emergency room at Madigan Army Medical Center several times, but nothing could be found. The doctors tried telling me that it was mostly stress related and I should slow down and take it easy.

I suffered with the pain for two years and yet the doctors still insisted it was nothing more than gas. I was given antacids to relieve the pain, but nothing worked. I noticed that the pain was worse after eating something and insisted that the doctors do something. After a series of test, they found I had gallstones and needed immediate surgery.

I had never been in the hospital except for when my children were born. And there was the time I was hospitalized after my fight with Gail when she cut me. But that was it. I was still scared of having surgery. It was considered a simple one, but I didn't want to go through it alone. Who would watch my children while I was away? Brad was gone at the time, but there was Allan and Angel to think about. They were too young to stay home alone and there was no one I could trust to stay with them. Except Bernice.

By that time, Bernice had five girls of her own. I hated to ask her to take on the responsibility of two more, but I had no other choice. She agreed to take Angel but thought Allan would feel out of place among so many girls. I had to turn to my dad as much as I didn't want to.

Much to my surprise, Dad agreed to take care of Allan. The day I was scheduled to go to the hospital, I stopped at Bernice's and Dad's to drop the kids off. Angel seemed excited to spend some time with Bernice's girls, but Allan appeared to be somewhat withdrawn. I could tell he didn't want to spend the time at Dad's, and I didn't blame him. I couldn't stand being in the house for an hour and yet, I had to leave my son in that environment for a week.

I checked myself into the hospital at one in the afternoon. Surgery was scheduled for the next morning. At ten that night, my nurse came to get me. I had an emergency call from Dad.

"What could he want?" I wondered.

"Barbara, Allan has run away. We don't know where he is."

189

What was I supposed to do from my hospital bed? I was due for surgery in the morning and was supposed to relax. Now my son was missing.

"Dad, don't worry, I am sure he will show up. I can't do anything from here."

No sooner did I return back to my bed when my nurse came to get me again to report I had another call. I hoped it was Dad to tell me Allan had returned but this time, Bernice was on the line.

"Allan showed up at my house tonight. He's very upset and worried about you. He said he wanted to be with Angel and asking to talk to you. Don't worry Barbara, he can camp out here until you come home." Then she put him on the line.

"Mom, I'm sorry. I just couldn't take it there anymore. I couldn't stand the arguing between Grandpa and Grandma. I could tell they didn't want me there. I'm sorry I made you worry."

He was crying and I wanted to put my arms around him and comfort him, but I had to settle for the right words over the phone line. I knew how it was living with Dad and understood how he felt. I should have never insisted he went there.

Surgery the next morning went smooth and without complications. My gall bladder was gone. I thought that the pain I had been suffering over the last two years would get better but the pain after surgery was far worse. I could hardly breath and the stitches burned and itched. I was told that if I did as I was instructed, I could go home in a week. The breathing exercises were the hardest. It hurt but I wanted to go home to my children more than anything. I worked through the pain. Every day, it was less and less severe and after about a week, I was able to go home.

Allan and Angel waited on me the best they could, only letting me do what they couldn't. They enjoyed taking care of their mother. I would make it up to them for the week I was gone. I knew after Allan ran away, that no matter what, I would not ask my dad for anything. He could do anything to me, but when he hurts one of my children, he would have to deal with me.

I knew there had to be more than a simple argument between Dad and Gail to cause Allan to take off. He didn't want to talk about it, but since that day, Allan refused the visit his grandparents unless it was necessary. I understood and never insisted he go with me. I didn't really want to go to that house either, but despite our differences, he was still my dad.

Chapter 25

Where There's Trouble, There's Brad

With Brad there was one crisis after another, as if Brad did the things he did to get the attention he seemed to need. Things got worse when he turned eight and Jim adopted him.

Brad thought Jim was his father, but because of the adoption, we had to tell the boys the truth. Brad turned on Jim suddenly, not wanting to follow Jim's rules and always yelling things such as:

"You're not my father; I don't have to listen to you!"

When we returned to Washington state, things got worse with Brad. He got involved with the wrong kids in school making it harder to control him than ever before. He would skip school and when I confronted him about it, he would make verbally abusive comments.

I used to think Brad followed the boys, so they would like him, but at times I wondered if he was the leader of the pack. I would find drugs and alcohol around all the time, hidden in cupboards and drawers. I would also find drug-related items hidden in his room. He always denied the things I found were his. He claimed it was always someone else's but he never had an explanation as to how it got there.

He was shoplifting with regularity or breaking into people's homes to steal anything of value. Anything he could sell to support his drug habit. Brad started stealing from my purse or taking my bank card without my knowledge. I tried everything, but nothing worked, until I decided that he needed to get away from his friends. After much thought, and acting on the advice of others, when

Brad was fifteen years old, shortly after Jim died, I turned my son into the authorities and watched them take him off to a home for juvenile delinquents.

Brad stayed at Echo Glen for a little over a year, coming home on occasional weekend visits. I made the two-hour drive to visit him often. I found that when Brad was away from us, he behaved and acted like the boy I wished he was when he was at home. When he was almost sixteen years old, they felt he was ready to live at home again.

Brad had decided to drop out of high school and needed something to do to fill in his time. The extracurricular activities he found still makes my skin crawl when I think back on that time.

As a teenager, the pranks became longer and more daring. Brad decided it was neat to watch the firemen put out fires. He decided they needed more practice. One day, shortly after he returned home from Echo Glen, he headed for a nearby field to set the dry weeds on fire. The distant sirens once again caused me to check on where they were going, wanting to believe that this time, it wasn't Brad. Hoping that the year away from us changed him, but the police escorting him home told me otherwise.

Then there was the time when Brad was fifteen. He was close to driving age and decided that he wanted to get a car that he can work on and have ready to drive by the time he was sixteen and had his license. I don't really recall how he did it, but he managed to strike a deal for a car through a friend. Imagine my surprise when the car was towed to our house and I realized that it was a hearse! It didn't run so he got it for free. How could I say no when I saw the pride on his face when he looked at it? He seemed to love that car, but I didn't know if he knew what the car had been used for. I wasn't going to tell him.

Brad was in the garage one day teaching Allan what he knew about fires. He seemed to be getting quite experienced with starting them. They were both striking matches, one at a time. Allan let one burn too close to his fingers and let it drop into a coffee can that had some gas in it. Once again, flames broke out. I was on the phone at the time. Apparently, Angel had witnessed the start of the fire and was the one to come get me. At the age of five, she ran in the house and tugged on my shirt to gain my attention. I kept pushing her away, telling her to wait until I was off the phone. She was persistent however and started crying, pointing out the kitchen window. When I looked to see what she was pointing at, I was horrified to see flames racing up the side of the garage wall, Allan and Brad standing outside just watching it. I hung up on my friend and frantically called the fire department. This time, the sirens were coming to us directly. When the fire was finally put out, we saw that the front of the hearse was a burned shell. So much for Brad's project car.

Brad grew from a teenager to a young adult. His large juvenile record was now sealed up. I hoped he would mature some and his clean adult record would give him the opportunity to start over. I hoped that he would change his ways but was naïve to dream it was possible. That he could mature and stay out of trouble because he's now an adult.

Brad continued to make bad choices on picking is friends. His best friend was Dwayne. They seemed to always be hanging out together. When they would argue or fight about something, the retaliation always made me cringe and fear what Dwayne might do.

One day when Brad was out, Allan, Angel and I were watching TV. Suddenly, the doorbell rang. There was a pizza delivery man standing on the step with a stack of pizzas. I was confused because we didn't order any

pizza. He showed us the order which did in fact have our
address. I started to turn him away when a taxicab pulled
up. The driver said he was called for a ride from my
address. Not knowing what to think, I told both the men
standing at my door that there must be some mistake.
Just then, a police car pulled up. A police officer jumped
out with his gun drawn followed by an ambulance and a
fire truck. Then it all started to become clear to me as I
saw the pizza delivery man and the taxicab driver with their
hands in the air, shaking and fearful with a stack of pizzas
littering the walkway. This must be the work of Dwayne.
When the police realized there wasn't any danger, he took
my statement. I told him I have no proof, but I think that
my son's friend, Dwayne might have something to do with
it. All the people and vehicles left, and all was silent once
again. Neighbors who had been watching the commotion
had all gone back to what they were doing. I have no idea
if they figured out for sure who made those calls or did
anything about it, but the pranks got worse.

On another late night, Angel and I had gone to bed
and Allan decided to stay up to watch TV. It was just past
midnight when I heard a loud bang that startled me awake.
I got up to see what was going on and found Allan sitting
on the floor, shaking. He pointed at the window. I was
horrified when I looked up to see a bullet hole in the glass.
I immediately called the police. When they questioned
Allan, I was shocked by what he told them. He was sitting
on the couch when a drive by shooter fired on the house.
The bullet came within inches of hitting Allan in the back of
the head. That was when I realized that I could have lost
my son that night.

When I saw Brad the next day, I told him I assume
Dwayne had something to do with the shooting and
demanded that he stop hanging out him. Brad said that he
and Dwayne got into a fight earlier that day. He wondered

out loud if maybe the bullet was meant for him. They must have worked out their differences because they continued as friends.

Brad was almost nineteen when I got a call from him. He was in jail. My first thought was, "What did you do this time?" He said that he did something stupid. He was hanging out with Dwayne who decided that it would be fun to rob a convenient store. During the robbery, Dwayne pulled out a gun. He said he didn't want any part of it once he saw the gun, but it was too late. The police arrived while they were still on the scene and they were both arrested. I wanted to help him out because he was my son. He has never been interested in guns so I'm sure he wanted no part in armed robbery if he could do it again. So, the next day, I drove to the bank, removed six hundred dollars which was almost all the money I had saved up and went to the Tacoma Corrections facility to bail him out. A decision I regretted soon after because it allowed him to be free to do what happened next.

Four years after Jim died, Brad had just turned nineteen, the sirens sounded one last time. Brad always did have a temper and it got out of control at a party one night at a friend's house. The host asked Brad to leave the premises because of his heavy drinking. Two hours later Brad returned to the house and set it on fire. The lights were out, and Brad thought the house was empty, but what he didn't know was a family of five were sleeping upstairs. A father jumped out the window first. The mother tossed their three young children out to him before she jumped out the window herself. Brad was later arrested for arson and attempted murder.

Brad was sentenced to twenty years. I watched them lead my son away in handcuffs, tears streaming down my face. I blamed myself for somehow failing my son. I cried for my first born, the little boy I cared for and loved. I fought to keep him when I was pregnant, went on the run with him, endured torture for fear he would be taken away, uprooted him several times just to survive. All that I did for him so that he could have a better life and I still couldn't protect him as he headed towards a life in prison. He was being taken away from me for years to come and at the time, all I could think of was... I failed my son and now it's too late. I remembered the promise I made to him years ago, when he was a baby. I would make things better for him and give him a better life than I had. I felt I'd broken my promise.

"I'm sorry." I whispered as my son vanished out of the court room into a waiting van to take him to prison.

As hard and frustrating as it was, I forced myself to pack the kids up and drive three hours to the prison in Monroe every month to visit Brad.

After the initial signing in at the front gate and going through a metal detector at the door, it did not appear to be like the prisons I had seen in the movies. There were no bars or glass windows between me and my son. I could hug him or hold his hand and know under the circumstances he was doing okay.

The visiting room was a large cafeteria with tables for visiting. There was a table of games so that the kids wouldn't be bored, and dozens of concessions stands if we got hungry.

The prisoners at the other tables were quietly visiting with their families and I silently wondered what each of them had done to be where they are now. As if reading my mind, Brad pointed out different men and told me tales of horror about each one. Rapists and child molesters seemed to make up most of the prisoners there. I cringed, knowing my son was forced to live among them.

Brad tried to assure me he was doing okay. He said he kept busy in the gym working out and that he was taking classes to get his high school diploma. I was proud of him. He was trying to change and again, it took strangers to do what I failed to do as a mother.

Two years after Brad was sent to prison, I received an invitation to attend my son's graduation from high school. Allan, Angel and I drove to the prison for the occasion.

The music started, and I saw my son walk down the aisle in cap and gown to receive his diploma. At that moment, I forgot that it was a graduation of prisoners. I only had eyes for my son as he tipped his cap in my direction and mouthed…

"I love you Mom."

After four long years, Brad was given parole for good behavior. He grew up in prison and as much as I hated for him to be away from me, Brad finally got the help he needed.

Ever since he's been free, the sirens have remained silent and hopefully they stay that way.

To my surprise, Brad found a job only a few weeks after being paroled and has worked ever since, living on his own, for a while. Eventually, he married a girl who had two boys. Then Brad became a father to a son of his own. Being a father himself now, he started asking questions about his real father. I did some research and believed to have found Lloyd's sister. After writing a letter to her and receiving confirmation that I found them, Brad moved his family to Arizona to where his father was now living. At last he got to meet Lloyd and his half-siblings.

Chapter 26

Along Comes BILL

1981

"Hello Barbara, this is Gloria."

It's been a long time since I've heard from Gloria. She was an old friend of the family, who at one time lived next door to us. I went to high school with her kids. She used to be a good friend of Gail's, but somehow throughout the years we became good friends despite the age difference. Though Gloria was almost twenty years older than me, she looked my age. She had tiny features weighing about one hundred and twenty pounds. Coal black wavy hair, dark tanned smooth skin. Although I knew her true age, the men she dated didn't. She never would admit her age, even to the department of licensing. I'm not sure how she did it, but her driver's license even left off about fifteen years.

Gloria's husband passed away the same year as Jim, and we found we had a lot in common. We both liked to go dancing and liked the same music so the two of us started going out together on weekly basis.

Neither of us drank alcohol. We lived on a natural high, dancing, partying, cruising around and flirting with the truckers on our CB radio. We loved following Vic around like he was the last man on earth.

Vic Trier was an Elvis impersonator who we became infatuated with and eventually became friends with. We followed him from club to club, always sitting at his table and sometimes even getting a free scarf that he would pass out to the ladies. I shivered the few times he made his way to me, slowly encircling my neck with a scarf as he sang a slow love song, anticipating the kiss I knew would come when he came to a break in the song. I had those scarves tucked away in my nightstand to remember that time long ago, finding myself wishing I could go back in time. Wishing that Vic was still around.

"Did I really want to repeat those years?" It was at one of Vic's shows where I met Bill.

I didn't notice him approach me until he was leaning on the table, asking me to dance. He wasn't very good looking but there was something about him that looked familiar, as if I had met him some other time, in some other place. We danced and told each other about ourselves, getting to know one another better in that short time on the dance floor. Before I knew it, we were dancing straight through several songs, not realizing it was getting late and the bar was preparing to close. Bill asked me to go for coffee with him down the street. There we talked until the early morning hours.

Bill had been in the army for twenty years and hoped to stay in for another ten. He was divorced with one grown daughter. Bill complimented me on everything. I found myself hypnotized by his flattering words. Jim was the last man to tell me I was beautiful, words I so longed to hear again. Though my head saw the red light, my heart ran through it, straight into trouble that I didn't see until it was too late to go back.

My friends warned me to beware, but I didn't listen. Someone was interested in me and if there was a chance for love again, I was going to grab it at any cost. For one-month, Bill wined and dined me, bringing me flowers and gifts. When he suggested moving in with me, I welcomed him with open arms.

Brad wasn't with us at the time, but Allan and Angel seemed to get along with him. Bill spent a lot of time with them and it seemed he would make a good stepfather. I was tired of trying to do everything by myself and needed some help, so Bill did not have to do much persuading for me to agree.

The first month he was there was wonderful. We would play games at the table and watch movies, always including the kids. Everything was wonderful, except the sex. I found myself once again pretending, as I did with Jim, to enjoy it. I found it much harder to pretend with Bill. He was rough and at times it hurt. He never seemed to care if I was satisfied or not, only satisfying himself before going to sleep.

In the second month, Bill started to complain that the house was too small and suggested we should move. I was hoping to have a permanent life with him, so I agreed to help look for a larger place. Something was always wrong with the houses we looked at. In a way, I understood how Bill felt, he was uncomfortable living in my house and wanted a place he could call his own.

One day, Bill brought up the idea of building a home. It sounded like a dream come true. I could plan every detail from carpets to appliances and everything would be new. Could we afford it? Bill said he could get a loan for his portion of the down payment and that the perfect way for me to help pay my half was for me to sell my house. I put it on the market that same week.

My house sold faster than we expected. We now realized we had no place to live while our new house was being built in Spanaway. The builders said to expect six months for completion, so we had to find someplace until then.

While reading the classifieds one day, I saw an ad from a couple who wanted house sitters for six months while they tried selling it. That sounded perfect, so I called them. When Bill came home that evening, we went to see the house. We moved in the following week.

As soon as Bill was out of my house, he started to change. The gifts stopped coming and the kids seemed to be in his way all the time. He would send them out of the room, not wanting to play games with them any longer. I didn't keep the house clean enough for him and my cooking didn't suit him, so he insisted on making all the meals. Bill was an army sergeant at work. Shouting orders was what he did, treating me and the kids like we were part of his troop.

Mommy's big REGRET #100

Bill insisted the house where we were temporarily staying was too small for the four of us and wanted to be alone without kids. He suggested we find somewhere for them to go while our house was being built. I went along with anything Bill wanted, afraid to defy him, and afraid that I would be alone again. I sold my home and all the money was put towards the new house. I had too much at stake to walk away now, so I put Bill ahead of my kids and agreed to find them a place to stay.

We found a place at Fort Lewis that had a small trailer park that was used as temporary housing for the incoming solders. Bill was confident he could arrange for the kids to stay there.

"Leave my kids alone, five miles away from me to fend for themselves?" I couldn't believe Bill would suggest such a thing! I reluctantly agreed. Anything Bill wanted Bill got!

As much as I was against it, the kids seemed excited about the prospect of being on their own, away from parental authority. Allan was a teenager by then and could watch out for his sister, I drove the distance every day to bring them food and take them to school. They seemed to love the time they lived in the trailer, or so I thought. The office at the park had a recreation room so they could play pool or video games to their hearts content. I missed them dearly, but Bill had changed towards them, so I sincerely thought it was best for them to be separated.

One month quickly turned into two. Bill and I were busy at the new home supervising the contractors, picking out the colors and planning the landscaping. In the third month, we were told the kids had to leave the park. They let the kids stay longer than legally allowed and they needed the trailer for other families, so they at last came home.

Having the house built was not as much fun as I anticipated it would be, because Bill and I could not agree on what we wanted. Bill had to have the best and the most expensive of everything in the house. I could not see why we needed such a fancy house and the expenses kept rising.

The house had two stories. Two bedrooms on the first floor and two on the second. There was two complete bathrooms, two fireplaces, a huge kitchen with an indoor bar-b-que grill on the top floor and a bar with its own kitchen on the bottom. We did save some money on the landscaping because Bill insisted on doing that himself, but still when the last of the bills came in, our house cost one-hundred and twenty-five thousand dollars!

As they promised, the contractors had our house finished almost six months to the day they started it. Moving day should have been a happy occasion, but by the time the house was completed, I was starting to regret jumping into this arrangement. I wanted out! I didn't know how to escape and so together, we signed the final papers and the house was ours.

I hated that house from day one. It was a masterpiece and under different circumstances, I would have felt like a queen living there. From the beginning, Bill let me know it was his house. I was not to cook or use "his" appliance's. He made sure the rest of the house was kept spotless.

Mommy Regret #101

Allan and Angel had no time for friends or homework. Bill made them scrub and clean from morning to night. He would not allow them in the front room or in any room he was in. If he was watching television in the recreation room, they had to go to their rooms. The hardest part, under Bill's watchful eye, was watching him turn my kids into slaves in the yard! Rain or shine he would wake the kids at seven in the morning, make them breakfast, and head the outside to start the landscaping. I knew he was a perfectionist in the house, but he was worse outside. Bill insisted every little rock was removed from the yard. The kids had to sift through the soil by hand using a contraption he built with wood and wire netting. They had to shovel the dirt onto the netting and push it around until every little rock was removed. If they missed just one rock, Bill would complain and make them redo their work. They were tired. Their hands blistered and callused, but he would not let up. I helped them as much as I can. I was afraid to speak up. Afraid I'd make things worse, so I kept quiet.

Two months after we were in our new home, I noticed another change in Bill, he started letting up on the kids and acted as though he could care less if the house was clean. He started staying out late or not coming home at all. I started cooking for the kids, something he never let me do before, suddenly, he didn't seem to care what I did. The first time he was out all night, I suspected there was another woman. My suspicions were confirmed when she

204

called for him one day. She told me they were an item and for me to get used to it!

If I cared for Bill at all, that call would have upset me, but I felt relieved, because I now had an excuse to leave. I would at last be free. Yes, I lost my home, my savings and all my furniture but I could start over. I've done it before and built up my life from nothing. I can do it again. I was mad because I realized Bill had used me to get him his house. He would not have been able to afford such a lavish home without my help. As soon as he had my signature on the papers, he started seeing someone else, which told me he never cared about me.

I was too afraid to confront Bill, so I quietly made plans to leave. I started by taking money out of the bank. Then I took my name off the account. The kids and I secretly packed, storing things under the beds until the day we would leave. I found an apartment on the other side of town in Tacoma and put a deposit down for them to hold it. When everything was done, I wrote Bill a goodbye note, pouring out everything I felt about him, holding nothing back, letting the tears flow. When Bill was at work we left and didn't look back.

I called Dad as soon as I was settled to give him my new phone number and told him what Bill did. He should have understood but his only comment was…

"Running away from your problems again, uh?"

By that time, Dad was alone. After a long illness, Gail had passed away. I thought for sure, now that he was no longer tied to Gail's apron strings, he would have needed me a little, but things didn't change for him. He was still the father I knew, belittling me, and ignoring his grandchildren.

I wondered what would become of the house Bill now lived in. Half of the house was mine and I hoped maybe I could force him to sell it and I would have a little money. After some investigating, I found out the woman Bill was seeing moved in one week after I moved out! I drove by there several times after that. I had to laugh to myself because I saw her in the yard sifting rocks!

After contacting a lawyer about the house several months later I discovered two things.

First, the value of the house was less then what we owed on it. If it were to be sold, by the time the creditors were paid off, we would not get any proceeds. Second, somehow, they had a quick claim deed signed by me, relinquishing all my rights to the house. What was wrong with that was I didn't sign anything! The signature looked like mine and I didn't have the attorney fees it would take to fight it.

I learned a very hard lesson that year. Not to trust any man again and never put a man before my children!

Chapter 27

The Truth Be Told

1990

When I left Bill's house, I never regretted it. The years after that were good to me and I kept my promise of not letting another man into my life. My friends didn't understand when I told them that I was happy without a man. To them, it wasn't natural to be alone and still be happy, but I was. I had my children and grandchildren and I had more friends than most married people did. I also had male friends who I went to breakfast with and occasionally dinner, but only as friends. Of course, in Dads mind, you can't have male friends without sleeping with them.

"It's not natural!" As he would tell me many times over.

After leaving Bills, the kids flourished and grew before my eyes. Allan found high school too difficult and dropped out in his junior year. I worried about that because I knew how difficult it would be to support himself without an education, but he proved me wrong. After taking a two-year cooking course at a vocational school, he found a job in a restaurant and moved out on his own.

After Brad came home from prison and found a good job, he moved to an apartment close by. It was at this time where he met Lore, a divorcee with two boys. After dating for a while, they were married on October twenty-fifth, 1991. Shortly After they presented me with my first grandson, Kyle. I fell in love with Lore's two boys, Josh and Eric. To me they were as much my grandsons as Kyle was.

I relaxed a lot after Brad's wedding, knowing that both of my boys were settled into lives of their own and my job was almost complete. Angel and I were at last alone, but I knew it would not be long before she was grown, and I was afraid I would no longer be needed as I was up until then.

I think I enjoyed Angel's teenage years more than she did. I lived them through her, seeing that she did all the things that I missed out on when I was her age. She was popular and had a stream of friends at the house all the time. Her friends seemed to prefer being at my house because they thought I was "real cool" and they didn't seem to mind that I would hang out with them. At times I wondered if I embarrassed Angel with the way I behaved in front of her friends, but she never said anything. I saw to it that Angel was able to join in any clubs she wanted, go to school dances, and when she was sixteen, I gave her a car, something I wanted as a teenager but never got.

The one secret I kept that haunted me as Angel was growing up ---- the story of her birth. I wrestled with telling her that Jim was not her biological father. I always felt that kids had a right to know where they came from.

Jackie was almost fifty years old and still didn't know what I learned a long time ago from Gail, that Dad wasn't her father. I swore that would never happen to my kids. Through the years I spoke to the boys about their fathers. Brad and Allan had both connected with Syd and Lloyd and are working on relationships with them. Angel's birth was different, and I never knew how to approach the subject. Jim and I talked about it at the time of conception. He couldn't have kids of his own so had asked for Angel to never find out. He didn't want his brothers to know of his infertility because he felt like, "Less of a man." And he didn't want Angel to know for fear that she wouldn't consider him to be her real father.

Angel had no memory of her father and I felt for medical reasons, if for no other reason, she should know the truth. Shortly after her sixteenth birthday, we had a long talk. I told her how much Jim and I loved her, how much we wanted to have a baby and how her dad's cancer made it impossible. Then I told her very gently of the very special person who donated the sperm that made it possible for us to get our beautiful daughter. As gentle as I was in telling her I saw the shock in her face and the tears in her eyes. After a moment of silence, she ran out of the house, away from me, and to her boyfriend for comfort. I wanted to hold her and tell her it made no difference, that her dad loved her, but I had to let her go. She needed to think for a while, to be alone. I knew she'd be alright. She was soon back to her old self and eventually able to speak of it openly to anyone who asked. I knew at times she wondered about the donor who gave her life, wondering if she looked like him, but she realized it was something we'd probably never know, and she had accepted it. To her, Jim was and always will be her dad.

Chapter 28

Off to College

While Angel was in high school, I decided it was time to do something for myself, so I enrolled in college. My days were filled with classes and homework. Because of the problems I had with Brad, I majored in psychology. I hoped that someday I could help other children in a way I couldn't with my own son. I loved the two years I spent in school, but though I improved my study habits since high school, I struggled to get passing grades. I was extremely proud the day I received my associate degree, but Dad was as usual, his pessimistic self, refusing to believe I could do anything right.

I started worrying about the kid's future without me. They were doing fine now, but I had nothing of value to give them when I passed on, so I decided to check into getting life insurance and called an agent for information. I was required to take a physical from their company and too my surprise was denied insurance. My urinalysis test was abnormal. I found that hard to believe because I was never sick, but because of the test I made an appointment at Madigan Army Hospital.

After weeks of test and x-rays, I was admitted to the hospital for a biopsy of my kidneys. When the results were in, my doctor called me into his office. I was diagnosed as having hereditary Nephritis (Alport's syndrome), the same disease that killed my mother! The doctor assured me that medicine has come a long way since Mom died and I could live a long happy life if I continue with routine checkups to make sure I don't start having symptoms. Years have passed since the diagnosis and I feel fine. Turns out I'm most likely just a carrier but was told I should have the kids checked out as well. Hopefully the disease will stay dormant. I am required to having yearly checkups and routine lab work, but I am fine.

My main concern was, "Will I pass it on to my children?" I followed the doctor's advice and had Angel checked out. The boys were both adults so all I could do was suggest they see a doctor and hope they will follow through. Angel did turn out to have the same abnormal urine screen as I did but also didn't develop any issues with it.

Alport syndrome is a genetic condition characterized by kidney disease, hearing loss, and eye abnormalities. People with Alport syndrome experience progressive loss of kidney function. Almost all affected individuals have blood in their urine (hematuria), which indicates abnormal functioning of the kidneys

Chapter 29

Dads Women After Gail

I couldn't cry for Gail, even though I knew her death would affect Dad. We were never close and selfishly, I hoped without Gail in the picture, he would reach out to me. Dad would once again be alone and maybe this time; he would need me. I hoped he could now become the father that I knew as a little girl. But Dad needed to have someone be dependent on him and insisted he was not meant to live alone. Within months after Gail's death, he started his search for someone else.

I couldn't help but remember the year Mom died. As much as he loved her, he couldn't wait until her grave was cold before he started looking for a new wife. I resented him for that. I felt if their love was as strong as he claimed, he would have waited a decent amount of time before marrying again. Now, with Gail gone, history was repeating itself.

Woman #1

Dad had hoped that my friend, Gloria would be his next wife, but she wasn't interested. He lavished her with gifts, took her to dinner and movies and stalked her! He would park his car down the street from her house and watch her nightly, making notes of where she went and who she was with. Gloria let him know it wasn't necessary to spend so much money and attention on her and told him flat out that she was not romantically interested in him, but he refused to listen. There was one good thing that came out of his pursuit of Gloria. Being my friend, she kept me informed on what he was doing.

I didn't think Dad wanted me to know about his private life, and if Gloria didn't keep me informed, I wouldn't have known how much he was spending on different women. First Gloria, then any other woman who came along. I was upset, because he couldn't spend a dime to help me, but he could squander his money on women he hardly knew!

I knew Dad couldn't get into trouble if he was spending time with Gloria, because she would report back to me. Dad realized in time that it was a hopeless cause to pursue Gloria and gave her an ultimatum. Marry him or he would move on. Even though she made it clear she couldn't marry him, they remained friends. As we had hoped, he still confided in her about everything he did.

It was through Gloria that I learned about the different girls he was throwing away his money on. Girls younger than me, who could only want one thing from a man three times his age… Money!

Woman #2

Gina was the worst of the girls he dated. She was a gypsy that he picked up from the street. Though Dad refused to admit it, she was a con artist, out to grab everything she could get her hands on.

She lived with her large family and from what Gloria told me, they acted and dressed like the gypsy's you would see in the movies. They told fortunes, read palms, and sold their wares on street corners, hustling customers and picking pockets to support themselves.

Dad opened an account at a furniture store and furnished her family's home. He bought Gina hundreds of dollars' worth of clothes. His credit cards were to the limit, so he borrowed from the bank to support Gina and her family.

Dad asked her to marry him and together they planned a huge wedding. The ring Dad bought her was filled with diamonds. I became angry about that because Dad could never afford to give mom the wedding ring she always wanted!

The wedding dress was white lace costing another thousand dollars on Dad's credit card. Dad paid for everything Gina wanted. The day before the wedding, Gina ran away with everything Dad bought for the wedding and married someone else!

It seemed Gina did what she did with the intention of marrying someone else all along, having Dad pay for her wedding. No one could say anything against Gina though, and Dad refused to believe he had been taken. As a reminder of what Gina did, Dad still paid the bills long after she disappeared.

Dad never confided in me about what Gina did and as far as I knew, he had no intention of having me at the wedding. Maybe he thought I would disapprove of spending all that money on a girl he hardly knew. I resented him at the time, because he couldn't help me pay the rent or feed my child when I begged him for help.

I thought Dad would've learned his lesson with Gina, but he jotted it down as a loss and continued on his way, in search of another wife.

Recalling how he met Gail, Dad once again started writing to girls in a singles magazine, and the letters once again started arriving.

Along came Ruth.......

<u>Woman #3</u>

Ruth was a divorced girl from Idaho who jumped at the chance of being the next queen in Dad's castle. From

214

the description Dad wrote about the house, he made it sound like something out of a magazine. Ruth couldn't wait to move right in.

She packed her belongings, drove to Parkland in her new sports car, full of anticipation, not knowing what she was coming to. Was she in for a rude awakening? Once she arrived, it was too late to turn back. It was her turn to face the old dilapidated house. It was without the garlic, but I'm sure she had the same reaction as Mom did when she first set eyes on it.

They were married in the ministers' front room, and to my surprise, I was invited this time. Maybe Dad thought I would approve of Ruth more than I would have of Gina.

I liked Ruth. We were close to the same age and had a lot in common, but she didn't need Dad in the way he wanted to be needed. She had her own car and didn't need him to drive her around. She was in good health and therefore, Dad had no one to take care of.

Ruth had hobbies and friends that she visited all the time. Dad felt left out. He wanted her to spend all her time with him. He wanted her to be his prisoner in his house and not be as free as she was.

Dad spent what money he had on her and paid off her high car payment. As soon as the car title was in Ruth's name, she too ran and filed for divorce.

Woman #4

Carol was the next women to enter Dad's life. She, like Ruth, came to Parkland hoping for a new start. Unlike Ruth, Carol was more dependent on him. She was a large woman who had a lot of health problems. Because she did not have health insurance, she had put off a much-

215

needed operation. Dad promised her free medical coverage in exchange for her devotion.

This time, Dad decided he could live with someone without a marriage license and Carol didn't seem interested in marriage, so she moved into Dad's house.

Carol lived with him for six months, and as he promised, Dad paid for her operation. She let Dad wait on her and support her while she recovered from her surgery. The day the doctor gave her a free bill of health, she packed her belongings. With the help of the congregation from Dad's church, she moved out. It turns out, she told them he physically abused her. These people who had known Dad and gone to church with him for over thirty years believed her.

I think after Carol left; Dad finally realized that women were using him for what they could get, and they didn't really care about him. He quit looking after that and decided he was better off alone.

I never understood why Dad felt he needed someone in his life so badly. He'd let just anyone move in and not once come to his own daughter who needed him. I would've loved getting the attention he gave to those women, and his grandchildren would've loved the attention he spent on strangers!

Chapter 30

So Long Dad

1992

I was skeptical the day Dad requested I come back home with Angel. He said he just wanted us to help him and keep him company. Moving back to my childhood home would be hard but it would help us save some money. We would not have any expenses, and I was hoping it help me heal old wounds. Hoping we could finally become closer.

Coming back here only brought up painful memories that I had tried to block out and seeing Dad now, I knew I could never forget them. I was the same girl I have always been, a little older and wiser but Dad only saw me the way he wanted to see me. As that clumsy little girl who could do nothing right. I felt he was waiting for me to screw things up again, but I was here to prove him wrong, to show him before he died that he was mistaken about me.

One day, Dad started having pains in his chest and his voice sounded hoarse. He was not one to complain and hated to go to doctors, but I saw the pain in his eyes. I finally convinced him to go to the hospital.

I felt that something was horribly wrong but was not ready to hear the results of his tests. Stage four esophageal cancer. It had metastasized to his lungs and liver. We were told he had a matter of months, maybe weeks left.

Dad didn't want to die in a hospital. He wanted to come to the home that he bought for Mom and his little chihuahua, Chi-Chi who he loved more than anything.

With the help of Hospice, Angel and I brought him home. A hospital bed was set up in the front room. We took classes on how to turn him, clean him and change his linens.

With Angel's help, we took care of Dad's daily needs, reading to him, turning him, just being there. He needed twenty-four-hour care. When Angel came home from work, we would change his diaper, roll him over and sponge bathe him.

On occasion, Angel and I would go outside to enjoy a warm breeze and relax, just needing a break from Dad. This was one of those nights. I was tired and my muscles ached from constantly having to turn Dad from side to side. I wanted to be out with my friends and forget about what was happening with Dad. Angel got up to head back inside to go to bed. She had to get up early in the morning for work, but I stayed outside awhile longer. It was too hot to sleep anyway and the light breeze coming my way felt too good to leave.

One night it was hot and humid. Sitting in the house was unbearable. I fixed a glass of lemonade for Angel and myself and the two of us went outside to sit on the porch. We were both tired and words went unsaid as we both sat there, each lost in our own thoughts. Although it's only been a couple of months that passed since I moved back, it seemed like I had been there forever, as if I had never left.

The birds were singing in the trees and the crickets were making their nightly noise. I suddenly shivered. I could have sworn I felt someone touch my shoulder. Through a haze, I saw my mom and Jim, hand in hand, reaching for me, smiling. I knew the two people I loved most in the world were together in eternity. My mother and my husband finally met and were trying to urge me on to finish the job I'd started. Letting me know that my journey was about to be completed. I felt more relaxed and ready for bed.

Dads nightshirt was wet from perspiration, so I took it off him. It was too hot to wear anything, and he would be more comfortable bare-chested. I gave him some ice chips, wiped his face with a cold wash rag, then headed to the bathroom for a cold shower.

For some reason, I slept better than I had in a long time. In my dreams, I saw mom and Jim encircling me with their arms, telling me how much they loved me. Angel's alarm interrupted my dreams. I heard her get out of bed and to the shower. It was only five in the morning, too early to wake up, so I rolled over and went back to sleep.

It was seven o'clock when I woke up. Jumping out of bed, I headed towards the kitchen to start the coffee. I was surprised to see Dad awake so early, but he was lying there staring at the ceiling, unaware that I was standing beside him. While the coffee was brewing, I returned to my room to get dressed and make the bed.

At eight o'clock, I changed Dad and gave him a sponge bath. I turned the television on for him and sat down to read the morning newspaper. Dad didn't seem interested in what was on the television, so I turned it off and started reading the paper out loud to him. Dad reached for my hand and made a soft groan. I had the feeling he was trying to tell me to stop reading, so I put the paper down and looked him in the eyes. I started speaking to him.

"Daddy, why couldn't you love me or show you care? There were many times when I needed you, but you were never there. Even when you were there, you ignored me. If I only knew what I did wrong to make you feel the way you did about me."

I wanted him to know, before it was too late, what he did to me. How much he hurt me and my children by his attitude toward us. So that morning, I poured my heart out to him, listing everything he did to me, making him remember those incidents as I was forced to remember them, not leaving one stone unturned.

"Remember the time when I came back from Salem? I turned to you for help. For a second you seem to want to comfort me, but Gail appeared, and the moment was gone. I never understood what power Gail had over you, that would make you turn against your own daughter! And the time when Gail told me about Jackie? I never forgave you for that. I was cut up and alone at the hospital after that fight and yet you blamed me. Dad, it would not have happened if you had been honest with me from the beginning and told me that Jackie was not your child. I would have understood. I loved mom dearly and nothing would have made me love her any less. Maybe I am as dumb as you accused me of being! Otherwise, why would I choose to come back to this house, to all these unpleasant memories."

An hour passed before I was through talking. I was out of breath, crying, feeling as if I said too much but with a sense of relief that I hadn't felt in a long time. I jerked with surprise as Dads' hand again reached for me and slowly gripped my hand. I looked into his eyes and was surprised to see tears slowly dripping from his eyes. I recalled the last time I ever saw Dad cry. It was the night Mom died, thirty years ago. He squeezed my hand now and I knew, he was trying to tell me he was sorry. At that moment, I realized it was time to bury the past. I looked at my dad and squeezed his hand in return as he slowly closed his eyes for the last time. His hand loosened its grip and fell to his side. I knew at that moment, Dad was gone. His pain was over, and my job was completed.

"Don't panic, Barbara." I told myself. I went to the telephone to retrieve the instructions the hospice nurse left me and read, do not call 911 or the police when the end comes, call your nurse. I picked up the phone and dialed.

"I'll be right there, Barbara." The nurse informed me. I couldn't stand to be in the house with Dad, so I went outside and sat on the porch just as Angel was pulling up the driveway. After I explained to her what happened, we sat together and waited for the nurse. She arrived thirty minutes later. While we stayed outside, she went in to check on Dad, confirmed his death and called the funeral home to come and get him. Angel and I remained outside, not wanting to go in the house. It seemed to take forever for Dad to be taken away. It was only after the hearse left that I could go inside.

I called my sister and a few relatives to tell them about Dad. There was a lot to do and I didn't know where not start. I couldn't bear to be in the front room with Dad's bed and the medical supplies lying around, so I remained in my room.

The nurse stayed behind, calling the medical suppliers to come and get the bed and equipment and to see what else she could do for me. I stayed in my room until everything was taken away and only then, did I leave my room. There was a lot to do but it could wait until tomorrow. After all these weeks of caring for Dad, I needed to take a moment before I faced dealing with the funeral arrangements.

Angel accompanied me to the funeral home and together we decided to have Dads body cremated, bring him home and at a more convenient time, have a service. Maybe by then, my sister could make the trip here to say goodbye. Dad purchased two cemetery plots in Longview, Washington when Mom had died, hoping he could someday be buried next to her. One month later, with my sister beside me, we buried Dads ashes next to Mom and said our final goodbyes.

After the service, Jackie went to Portland to spend the night at my aunts before heading home to California. I went in the opposite direction, back to Tacoma.

The telephone rang the next day. Aunt Mae was on the other end apologizing. "Barbara, I did something terrible. I didn't mean to, but I thought she knew." My aunt sounded upset. What could she have possibly done?

"By accident, I mentioned the fact that your Dad was not Jackie's father. She didn't know! I can't begin the describe the look on her face. Please forgive me."

"It was way past time she knew, please don't blame yourself. Maybe you were the only one who did the right thing. Jackie had a right to know."

Now I knew, after many years of wondering, that my sister didn't know who her father was.   Not knowing weather Jackie knew the truth, wondering what she was thinking, wishing I had been the one to tell her had been agonizing for me. She was fifty years old and never suspected what the rest of us knew. How could Dad keep such a thing from her? But then again, if Gail hadn't told me, I think just maybe the secrets of Mom's past would have been buried with him, because I doubt if Dad would have ever told us the truth himself.

Chapter 31

Finally, At Peace

The house was quiet now that Dad was gone. I found more time on my hands than I really wanted. Time to think without interruptions and nothing to do to keep my mind from racing. I rearranged the furniture back to the way it used to be and cleaned up the yard. The leaves were turning brown and falling to the ground, telling me that fall was here, and winter would soon arrive.

Dads belongings were still in every room. I knew that I couldn't put off going through his things much longer. I found copies of his life insurance policies, and bank account statements. His financial matters need to be taken care of first. He had outstanding debts and burial expenses that were overwhelming. I hoped there would be enough left over for repairs to the house, but there wasn't.

Then there was the chore of going through Dads' clothes. Most was old and torn, but I bagged everything up as it was and called a shelter to pick it all up. There must be a need for the clothes no matter what shape they were in.

I decided to continue living with Angel in the house, regardless of how I felt about the place. It would help not paying rent, and I was sure no one would want this old rundown place. The house was in bad condition and although I wouldn't have rent since the house was paid for, the repairs would cost me a fortune. The furnace gave out and had to be replaced, and the stove needed attention. The roof leaked, and there were drafts in every corner of the house, so the heating bill was outrageous. I didn't know what I was going to do. I couldn't afford staying here and I couldn't afford to move either.

I was trying to clean up the house the best I could considering how run down every inch of the house was when the phone rang.

"Barbara, my son wants to talk to you." Gloria informed me.

What could he want? Though I went to high school with Raymond, I hadn't seen him in many years.

"Would you available to meet with him tomorrow?"

I told her I would be home, but I was curious as to the nature of the meeting, racking my brain, wondering what it could be about.

"I guess I'll have to wait till tomorrow." I told myself, putting it in the back of mind. Afterall, I had a lot more work to do to get this house in order.

In the morning, Raymond arrived earlier than expected. He told me he wanted to make me an offer on the house!

"You know I'm a contractor, although the house is not worth a lot I would like to invest in the land. If you consider selling it, I'm prepared to pay twenty-five thousand dollars."

"You really want to buy this place?" I asked in astonishment. "Please let me think it over."

But what was there to think about? I would be a fool not to sell, a part of me wanted to hold on to the last thing I had of Mom's. I could see her standing in the yard on the first day Dad showed it to her, staring at the garlic in disgust, ready to strangle him. Even with all the bad memories, there were a few good ones. How could I let it go?

As if the offer Raymond made me didn't throw me for a loop, my neighbor came over to chat. I casually mentioned the offer Raymond made me and asked for his advice. He too, was a contractor and had purchased a few houses as rentals. I figured he would know if the price was right. Before I knew it, he made me an offer as well. Jumping the price up to thirty-thousand dollars. If he bought the place, he would own everything on the street. A house I thought nobody would want now had two buyers eagerly fighting over it. Each trying to outbid the other. Raymond withdrew his offer and I sold it for forty-thousand dollars.

Before I could close the sale, I had to get the paperwork together, so the deed was free and clear in my name. I got a lawyer to assist in settling Dad's estate and found out a few things I didn't know before.

There were two things that kept me from obtaining the deed to the house that I wasn't aware of. The house was owned by both Dad and Gail. I never knew Dad had put Gail's name on the deed. According to the lawyer, Dad did that the year he married Gail. To make matters worse, in Gail's will, she left everything she owned to her two daughters. This meant her daughters owned half the house! I was fuming! What right did Gail have to Mom's house? And what right did she have to give it to her daughters?

The lawyer assured me there wouldn't be a problem if the daughters relinquished the rights to their half. He wrote letters to each with forms for them to sign away their rights. One was returned without hesitation, but the other daughter held out. I didn't understand why. The house had no value to her. She had nothing to gain by keeping it but for a month my lawyer and hers battled it out, trying to settle it. In the end we won, and she signed her share away.

225

Now that the ownership was settled, there was one other problem. Dad had large outstanding bills which I knew nothing about, and the creditors held a lien against the house. It was decided we would sell the house to the neighbor and give all the money to my attorney. He paid off the creditors, took his lawyer fees, and I would get what's left over.

When everything was done and all the paperwork completed, I was given my share of the money. Out of forty-thousand dollars, I was handed a check for half that amount. It took twenty-thousand dollars between the creditors and lawyer fees.

I now had to decide the best use for the money and where I was going to live.

I couldn't afford to buy another house or make payments on one, so I took the money and bought a mobile home. I had to be out of the house in two weeks which seemed impossible. Dad had thirty years of items accumulated and I had no idea what to do with everything.

I divided the dishes and other kitchen items to give to Brad and Allan. They took what they wanted, and the rest went to the Goodwill. In my mind, I was giving back to an organization that helped me in my time of need all those years ago.

It was a busy week, but things were getting done faster than anticipated. Most everything Dad owned had showed its age and had to be thrown away.

By the end of the week, all that was left was to pack my own things. Most of it was in storage so it didn't take long. I needed my suitcases which were stored in Dads' closet, so I headed off to retrieve them. As I stood on tiptoes to reach the furthest corner of the closet, I felt an envelope and pulled it out, thinking it was just more garbage to throw away. The envelope was hard and bulky and addressed to me, in Dads own handwriting.

"What could this be?" I thought to myself.

I sat on the bed, staring at it for a moment. Then I tore open the envelope, inside was a tape recording. On the label were instructions that said, "Do not open until my death. Dad."

I was curious and wanted to play the tape but was afraid to. Knowing Dad, it was probably instructions on his burial because even in death, Dad would think I was incapable of doing things right and needed to have the last word. There was still a lot to do and I didn't have time to deal with this right now. I dropped the tape into my purse and continued packing.

Moving day was made a lot easier, thanks to friends who showed up with their trucks. Before noon, I was ready to hand the keys over to the neighbor. I hesitated in the yard for only a moment, saying goodbye to my childhood and to Mom. Before I drove off, I stopped at the maple tree Mom planted the day we moved in and engraved her name into the trunk of the tree and added the date she planted it.

"For you mom," I said and with that, I drove off to my new home.

The rest of the month, Angel and I kept busy settling into the mobile home. I forgot completely about the tape inside my purse. One day, while reaching for my check book, I came across it once again and decided it was time that I listen to it. I inserted it into a small tape recorder, cuddled up on the sofa and prepared myself to listen to Dad's voice for the last time.

Hello lovely daughter, Barbara. This is my final request to you on my demise. I wish to be cremated at Dryers Funeral Home. They will take care of the details. Please make sure they bury them with your mom in Kelso. I have a gravesite there. If and when you see fit, please put a marker there. You have heard many stories about me, much weren't true. I swear to God; I have never done anything wrong. God knows I love you and the kids very dearly. We don't always agree on that. I understand you have your own life to live. You have your own way to go, therefore you couldn't always look after me. Look through my papers and so forth. I'll try to have them all in order. Take my titles and everything and send them in as soon as possible and get them in your name in case I have any debts unpaid. No debtors can claim anything. I have no mortgage on my house. I never had and never will have. I've never signed anything. If you're not around, all the above goes to Brad. He is named on my insurance. I love you very much. I hope you didn't believe the many lies told on me. Love Dad

I slammed the off button on the recorder, not wanting to replay his message again. Wanting to let go and love him. It was over and it was time to move on. I forgave my dad on his deathbed and realized I could forgive him now. We were both finally at peace.

Epilogue

The bad times were thankfully behind me. As I reach my golden years, those are what I wish to remember. Although they were few and far between, I hope I gave you some laughter to compensate for the tears.

My best memories besides my children is my life with Jim. It's been forty-two years without him but to me it seems like only yesterday. I see his picture when I go to bed at night and when I wake in the morning. I tell him good night and I almost feel him next to me as I go to sleep.

The children are grown now with families of their own. They are no longer children, but adults. Despite the hardships of their past, became stronger because of it.

Brad realized his mistakes and hugs me often. Many times, he has shown me, not in words but actions, how sorry he was. I had said that I regretted bailing him out if jail, making him free to start the fire that sent him prison, but I later realized it was the best thing that ever happened to him. Prison woke him up, aged him, changed him. He became a son I was proud of. Shortly after he got out of prison, he found job and has worked steadily ever since. He met and married Lore and became stepdad to her two boys, Josh who was six and Eric was one. I became an instant grandmother as if they were my own flesh and blood. Kyle came along a few years later. The family was growing. Unfortunately, the marriage ended bitterly, but the boys stayed in touch. Josh and Eric will always be a part of the family, my grandsons. Brad lived in Arizona to be close to his dad for years, getting to know him. Lloyd had since passed away and Brad moved back home after the divorce. He now lives in Port Orchard, Washington with his girlfriend. He paid me a visit this last Mother's Day, we had a good visit, but I couldn't help noticing. My first born was turning gray and I was turning old! Josh has a wonderful family with three kids of his own. He is living in Jacksonville, Florida. I hear from him often. Eric lives in El Paso, Texas with his wife and two kids. Kyle lives in Dallas, Texas with his wife and their eighteen-month-old son Hamza. All three of them still call me Grandma as that is what I am. Not quite sure however if I'm ready to recognize the title of Great-Grandma.

Allan was my quiet, shy boy. He is soft spoken, never stressed, never raises his voice. He had a lot of trouble in high school and dropped out in his junior year. He never received his high school diploma, but he enrolled in vocational school at the age of eighteen to become a cook and has worked ever since. He has been a chef at a casino for many years. That is where he met his wife Carol. Carol had grown children from a past marriage, but Allan never had children of his own. A few years ago, they adopted Carol's three-year-old grandson, Isaac. Allan finally became a dad. They were allowed to change his name as part of the adoption agreement, so Allan was able to pass on to him his last name but as a tribute to the only dad he knew growing up, he gave Isaac the middle name of Kenneth which was Jim's first name. I found Syd and introduced him to the son he never knew he had. He lives in Walla-Walla. Allan went there every year to visit his dad and get to know his new family until Syd started developing dementia and had a hard time recognizing his son. I think that was hard on Allan, so he stopped his annual visits to see him. I'm just glad he got to know his dad while he was still the Syd that I remembered.

Angel said the events that led her to her career choice stemmed from Dad's passing. The time she spent caring for him in his last days sparked something in her to want to take care of people. Angel is a registered nurse at a local hospital. It took her along time to get where she is today, but she did it on her own. She worked first at Kmart, then at Sears. While at Sears, she met the father of her son, Christian. Though they parted ways, together they co-parented and raised their son. Angela went on to community college to study to become a nurse while I helped her take care of Christian. Christian was four when she met Mike and married him five years later. A few months after her daughter Emily was born, I saw her graduate and receive her nurses pin. Two years later Erin joined the family, by then Christian was thirteen years old. They have a nice house, good income, and great kids. They just bought twelve acres of property and are preparing to build their dream home. (I often wonder if the kids were related to me) maybe it took a generation or two to get it right.

Christian graduated High School with honors. Two days later, he graduated from Pierce College with an associate degree through the running start program. Four years later, he graduated from the University of Washington with a degree in community and environment planning. The first four-year college graduate in my family! He has a great job and keeps in touch often.

My children are near, and I see them often. I'm glad they let me share their life with you. They had no idea of where they came from or what I had been through to get to this place until they read my story within these pages.

My senior years are here. I'm living in a Shag senior living apartment. I have lots of friends and love all around me. It may have taken nearly sixty years, but I found a life that I should have had from the beginning. I am ready to start a new chapter of my life.

Acknowledgements

2019

I would like to thank my children for putting up with me all these years while I work on my thoughts and putting them down on paper. To Brad, thank you for letting me tell your story, without you I would only have a partial story to tell, or the grey hair that came with being your mom. To Allan, my middle son, so quiet I never knew what you were up to. I am sure a few of these grey hairs came from you.

Thanks to my beautiful daughter, Angela for proofreading, correcting my English and spelling and doing the pictures, also for putting up with my nagging to help me complete this book.

Thankyou Bernice for being there for all my ups and downs in my life, for always being my friend.

To my sister Jackie, though we're far apart, you're always in my heart. (In 2018, The doctor finally removed the BB from my shoulder. I kind of feel lost without it.)

To my friends, too numerous to mention, thanks for your friendship.

And to my dear Husband Jim, no longer with me, but always in my thoughts. Without you showing me what love was all about, I would never have the courage to write this book.

Love to you all

CPSIA information can be obtained
at www.ICGtesting.com
Printed in the USA
LVHW090518250320
651141LV00002B/440

9 781686 653599